# How to Increase the Value of Your Home

# How to Increase the Value of Your Home

**VICKI LANKARGE**

**DANIEL J. NAHORNEY**

McGRAW-HILL

NEW YORK   CHICAGO   SAN FRANCISCO   LISBON   LONDON   MADRID
MEXICO CITY   MILAN   NEW DELHI   SAN JUAN   SEOUL
SINGAPORE   SYDNEY   TORONTO

The *McGraw·Hill* Companies

1 2 3 4 5 6 7 8 9 0 DOC/DOC 0 1 0 9 8 7 6 5 4

ISBN 0-07-143693-6

This publication is designed to provide accurate and authoritative information in
regard to the subject matter covered. It is sold with the understanding that neither
the author nor the publisher is engaged in rendering legal, accounting, or other
professional service. If legal advice or other expert assistance is required, the services
of a competent professional person should be sought.
—From a Declaration of Principles jointly adopted by Committee
of the American Bar Association and a Committee of Publishers.

McGraw-Hill books are available at special quantity discounts to use as premiums and
sales promotions, or for use in corporate training programs. For more information,
please write to the Director of Special Sales, McGraw-Hill Professional, Two Penn
Plaza, New York, NY 10121-2298. Or contact your local bookstore.

This book is printed on acid-free paper.

Library of Congress Cataloging-in-Publication Data

Lankarge, Vicki.
    How to increase the value of your home : simple, budget-conscious techniques
and ideas that will make your home worth up to $100,000 more / by Vicki Lankarge
and Dan Nahorney.— 1st ed.
        p.    cm.
    Includes index.
    ISBN 0-07-143693-6 (alk. paper)
    1. Dwellings—Remodeling. 2. Dwellings—Remodeling—Cost-effectiveness.
3. Dwellings—Valuation. I. Nahorney, Dan. II. Title.
TH4816.L333 2004
643'.7—dc22

                                                           2004005634

FOR JANET, ELIZABETH, KRISTEN, AND STEPHEN

– DJN –


FOR DENNY, DAVE, AND MARIE

–VL –

# Contents

## GIMME SHELTER: PROTECT YOUR INVESTMENT

## HOME RESOURCES

# Acknowledgments

**W**ithout the generosity of so many individuals, this book would not be complete. Dan and I would like to thank Mary Glenn, our editor at McGraw-Hill, for helping us shape this book and the amazing home professionals (and the people who work with them) for sharing their time and expertise with us. They are: David Adams, Dan Blitzer, Jim Cory, Janet Carter, Bob Clements, Chris Davis, Sean Farmer, Steve Gladstone, Alan Hanbury, Steve Hendy, Tiffany Keaton, Larry Lauck, Larissa Marsh, A.J. Paron-Wildes, Tony Paulos, Jeanne Salvatore, Barbara Schwarz, Carl Seville, Sue Smith, Edward Stevens, and Don Woods.

We'd also like to acknowledge several organizations and businesses that provided us with consumer information for this book, including the Insurance Information Institute, the National Association of the Remodeling Industry, the World Floor Covering Association, and the World Lighting Association. A special thanks goes to Sal Alfano, editor of *Remodeling*, a Hanley Wood publication, for permission to use data from the magazine's 2002 and 2003 *Cost vs. Value* report. A nod also goes to the National Association of Realtors and the National Fire Protection Association for producing terrific Web sites chock full of good consumer information. (See Chapter 14 for a list of Internet addresses.)

Personally, I'd like to thank my coauthor, Daniel J. Nahorney, for helping to make this experience such a rewarding one. For me, the process of writing this book with Dan pleasantly reaffirmed what I already knew from our days writing together at *insure.com*: We work extremely well together.

Most importantly, I'd like to thank my husband, Ken, and my children, Matthew and Annelise, for their love, laughter, and support. Guys, you know I couldn't do it without you.

Finally, I'd like to say that no one has taught me more about the true meaning of the word "fidelity" than my brothers and sister, to whom this book is lovingly dedicated.

— VL —

I would like to thank my wife, Janet, for her constant, unwavering support. She, along with my children, Elizabeth, Kristen, and Stephen, helped to make this book a reality. I'd also like to thank my parents, John and Florence Nahorney, who have encouraged me to write ever since I was able to hold a pencil.

A special thanks also goes to Dan Fontaine for his insightful editing. I'd also like to say that Vicki Lankarge is just a pleasure to work with. She understands and epitomizes the true meaning of teamwork.

— DJN —

# Introduction

**H**ome improvement is our new national pastime. My coauthor Vicki and I can say that unequivocally because of one stunning fact: Consumers spent a record $163 billion on home improvements in 2002, and that was easily surpassed in 2003, as they sunk more than $200 billion into their homes.

This trend has spawned all kinds of "how to" books. How to build a deck, how to fix your kitchen, how to wire a house, and how to fix your plumbing. But our book is a little different. It's a "how to" book that shows you how to tackle home improvements so that you actually increase the value of your home.

This book will help you decide where to start. Should you begin in the kitchen with the dark brown cabinets, the dark brown burlap on the walls, and the ceiling fixture with two 15-watt light bulbs? Or perhaps in the formal dining room with the black spiral staircase? Or the front hallway with the closet painted like a circus tent with alternating chartreuse and white stripes?

Don't laugh. I was faced with remodeling all three. The first two have come and gone, but I just won't let my wife Janet paint that closet. That's because when we get compliments about our house, I want people to know that it didn't always look the way it does today. Having a book like this when we first started our home remodeling odyssey would have saved us from some early mistakes.

Vicki's situation is a little different. She has yet to embark on her remodeling adventure. But with a house measuring less than 1000 square feet, one bathroom, two kids, and a husband looking for some small corner of the house to call his own, believe me, she has more than just a professional interest in this subject.

If you're like us, your home is probably your largest asset—the same as it was for our parents and grandparents. The biggest difference is that during the past 50 years, a few digits have been added to the value of most homes in the United States. Today, the average home sells for approximately $170,000. In some areas, such as metropolitan San Francisco and Boston, homes sell for an average of $560,000 and $410,000, respectively. So when you decide to embark on home improvements, you are actually working on increasing the value of your biggest investment. And you should always thoroughly plan for any large financial commitment you are about to make, particularly when it involves your home.

Why? Because the average person in the United States moves about every seven years. So if you're considering some serious home improvements, you might be putting $20,000, $30,000, $60,000 or more into your home. But if you choose the wrong project, you will get precious little of that money back when it comes time to sell.

Take swimming pools, for example. Say you decide to invest $30,000 in an in-ground pool because you love swimming and many of your neighbors have a pool. But three years later, when your company relocates you halfway across the country, instead of adding $30,000 to the value of your home, you find that the pool only adds $14,000. And to make matters worse, your real estate agent informs you that several prospective buyers don't even want to see your home because of your pool and the increased liability that comes with it.

This book is designed to help you decide which projects will give you the biggest bang for your buck. We also provide you with tips that come in handy before, during, and after your projects. That's because it's not a matter of whether you will embark on home improvements. It's a matter of when, how many, and at what cost. Home improvement stores such as Home Depot and Lowe's have sprouted up across the nation. Just try to find a parking space within reasonable walking distance of their front doors—and not just on weekends, but weekday nights as well. With mortgage rates hitting 40-year lows in 2003, the number of people who refinanced their mortgages and took out additional cash will fuel a mass of home improvements for years to come. But what improvements should you make with that cash? And how much should you spend?

Well that depends. We will offer some guidelines, but unfortunately there are no hard-and-fast rules that cover each and every home in every neighborhood across the country. If you are most concerned about getting the maximum amount back on your home improvement, then you should use this book as a guide, and do some additional homework on your own.

If you're going to plow ahead with a home improvement despite what it will do to your resale value, you can use this book to help you make minor adjustments to your plan to ensure you get back as much as possible. For example, Dan's pool is above ground and would require much less work to remove than would an in-ground pool.

So pools are bad investments, but you love being outdoors. What else can you do? If you enjoy sitting in your back yard at night, but you hate mosquitoes, you might want to think twice about adding a deck. Although decks were popular in the 1980s and 1990s, homeowners are now expanding their living space by putting roofs over them and adding screened rooms complete with plants, comfortable furniture, and dinner tables. (We've come full-circle here. Seventy years ago, homes were commonly built with screened-in porches.)

Not interested in the outdoors, but want a bigger bedroom because you're sick and tired of shuffling around your bed to avoid crashing into pieces of furniture? By all means, add on! But for maximum resale value, you should seriously consider adding at least one walk-in closet. And don't forget the master bath.

Times indeed have changed. The homes our parents and grand-parents lived in were worth less, but our relatives didn't seem to mind so much back then. First-generation families often lived in four-room apartments, one bedroom of which was shared by three, four, or five children. Today? Children feel deprived if they don't have their own room, complete with television, telephone, and computer (with high-speed Internet access, of course).

Our parents relaxed watching Uncle Miltie, Ed Sullivan, and Lucille Ball. Today's parents relax watching HGTV, *Trading Spaces*, and Bob Vila's *Home Again*—and the home improvement show *While You Were Out* is even popular with teenagers.

Homes used to provide basic shelter and a warm hearth around which you gathered your family. Today they are showpieces. Home improvement used to mean choosing a new color to paint the living room. Today, it's building a new family room. Remember when you redecorated the kitchen by putting up new wallpaper? Forget it. Now you knock out a wall and add a center island, new cabinets, granite countertops, and radiant heat beneath the new tile floor—more than doubling the size of your kitchen, even though take-out is more popular than ever.

So if you are dreaming of your next home improvement project and can't wait to call the architect or take a trip to Lowe's, hold off for just a bit. You can start by getting comfortable, grabbing a pencil, and taking the quiz in Chapter 1. Turn the page, and together let's figure out where and how you should get started.

# How to Increase the Value of Your Home

# PART 1

# LAY THE GROUNDWORK

*"Remodeling is like open-heart surgery: It's painful, inconvenient, and not the most pleasant experience to go through. You need to stay focused on the end result." – Paul Zuchs, president of the award-winning design/build firm Capital Improvements, Allen, Texas.*

# CHAPTER 1

# WHAT'S YOUR REMODELING PROFILE?

# QUIZ: SHOULD YOU REMODEL OR SELL?

One of the most nerve-wracking aspects about remodeling to increase the value of your home is this: Should you spend all this money on home improvement or just sell your house as it is and start over? Before you embark on any extensive improvement project, it's a good idea to determine whether remodeling is the best option for you, or whether it makes more sense to buy another house that will better fit your needs.

The following questionnaire, courtesy of *ourfamilyplace.com*, will help steer you in the right direction. Answer each question and record the number of points associated with that answer.

1. **How far "off" is your present house from the one you would like to live in?**
   - A little (5)
   - Somewhat (3)
   - A lot (1)                          Score: _____

2. **What are the property values doing in your neighborhood?**
   - Increasing (5)
   - Staying the same (3)
   - Decreasing (1)                    Score: _____

3. **What are property conditions doing in your neighborhood?**
   - Getting better (5)
   - Staying the same (3)
   - Declining (1)                     Score: _____

4. **How long will you get useful life out of any potential remodeling?**
   - 10+ Years (5)
   - 3–10 Years (3)
   - Less than 3 Years (1)                    Score: _____

5. **In relation to your house, the other homes in the neighborhood are:**
   - Larger (5 )
   - Similar (3)
   - Smaller (1)                              Score: _____

**TOTAL:** _____

Let's take a look at your results. If you scored under 10 points, moving might be your best option because you know you're not going to own your current home for long and you might live in a neighborhood where the property values are actually decreasing.

If your total is between 10 to 17 points, either option (moving or remodeling) might work for you. You need to take other factors—such as your budget and your job stability—into consideration.

Any score of 18 or above indicates that remodeling might indeed be a good idea, especially if you are committed to your neighborhood and the property values where you live are stable or increasing.

Even if you've already decided that it makes sense for you to remodel, don't call the lumberyard just yet. Next you have to look at whether you need to repair before you remodel. Even if you've decided to sell without remodeling, hold off for a bit before you call a real estate agent. While repairs might not increase the value of your home, maintenance left undone can take dollars out of your pocket at resale.

# CHAPTER 2

# REPAIR BEFORE YOU REMODEL

# ARE YOU LAZY
# ABOUT HOME MAINTENANCE?

Imagine sitting down in a first-class restaurant with elegant decor and impeccable service. You know that your filet mignon will set you back $25, but you don't mind. You value this establishment's fine ambiance. Then you take a closer look. Your crystal water goblet is spotted. Your utensils are crusted with bits of leftover food. And there's a bug scaling the peaks of your artfully folded napkin. *Now* how much would you pay?

You would pay nothing because you would have already bolted for the door. No customer willingly pays extra for candles and a smartly dressed maitre d' if the restaurant can't provide even the most basic level of sanitation.

So it goes with remodeling your home. You can't expect a potential buyer to shell out your asking price, based in part on that brand new gourmet kitchen with the whisper-quiet dishwasher, if you've never updated the insufficient electrical service to your home. Any competent home inspector will tell your prospective buyer that this impressive new appliance is tripping circuit breakers every time you run it.

Although fixing the basics doesn't always add to the value of your home, you can be sure that repairs and routine maintenance left undone will hurt your bottom line when it comes time to sell. Minor problems can quickly become nightmares, especially where wet basements, rot, or pest infestations are concerned.

Most homeowners are lackadaisical about home maintenance, but it's not because they're lazy, according to Stephen Gladstone, president of the American Society of Home Inspectors (ASHI). Homeowners often ignore routine maintenance and repairs because they feel safe and secure in their own homes. "But it's really a false

> **TIP:** *Before you remodel, dust off that old home inspection report—you know, the one the bank made you get when you first bought your home. Are there any remaining maintenance or repair issues that you haven't yet addressed? Also, if you've owned your home five years or more, you might want to consider hiring a home inspector to come in again and take another critical look to uncover any potential problems that might decrease the value of your home at resale.*

sense of safety," he says. "No one is going to warn you when something in your home is about to go wrong. There's no knock on the door: 'Hi, I'm your gutter and I'm full. Now clean me.'"

# THE TOP 10 MOST COMMON HOUSE PROBLEMS

Before you decide on a fresh new color scheme or whether your remodeling budget can encompass a whirlpool, you must first identify repairs or deferred maintenance that need to be done. Does your home have a damp crawl space? Are there an insufficient number of electrical outlets? Do your windows and doors stick?

According to ASHI, these are just a few of the top 10 most common house problems. It is noteworthy that within ASHI's list of 10 problem categories, at least 4 are directly related to the damaging effects of water—the element, says Gladstone, "that drove humans into the caves in the first place."

Keeping water out is the homeowners' most important and continually challenging task. This is because water is mold's best friend. Within 24 to 48 hours after water has invaded your home, mold can begin growing on water-soaked material, such as walls, floors, carpeting, books, clothes, and furnishings. And, unless you've been living under a rock for the past two years, you've surely heard that "toxic" mold can devastate your health and your home. (For more information, read *What Every Homeowner Needs to Know About Mold*, by Vicki Lankarge, McGraw-Hill, 2003.)

Today's homebuyers are very educated. They will not be bowled over by your remodeled basement with a home theater if they also notice the water stains around your basement windows. So in order to get the most bang for your remodeling buck, you must first address any maintenance and repair issues. According to ASHI, the top 10 most frequent house problems are:

1. *Grading and drainage problems.* Improper surface grading and drainage lead to damp basements or crawl spaces. The most effective remedies for wet basements include regrading the ground away from your home and repairing or installing a new system of roof gutters and downspouts.

2. *Improper electrical wiring.* Insufficient electrical service to the house, inadequate overload protection, and amateur wiring connections are also common home defects. According to ASHI, much of the electrical wiring that is done improperly is directly attributable to do-it-yourselfers. This is a serious safety hazard because poorly installed wiring can start an electrical fire.

3. *Roof damage.* Roof leakage, caused by old or damaged shingles or improper flashing, is also a frequent house problem. While shingle repairs can be easily and inexpensively done, shingles near the end of their life span might signal the need for roof replacement, a major expense. (See "A Word about Roof Replacement" at the end of this section.)

4. *Older or poorly maintained heating and cooling systems.* From blocked chimneys to unsafe exhaust disposals to leaking water heaters, these are all problems that stem from neglected heating and cooling systems. Heating systems should be

serviced annually by a professional, according to the manufacturer's instructions. Most homeowners take for granted their furnaces, water heaters, and air conditioners—until they stop working. Then there's the panicked emergency call to the plumbing and heating contractor on a Sunday afternoon that is not only costly, but in most cases, entirely avoidable—*if* the appropriate maintenance had been performed in the first place.

5. *Older or poorly maintained plumbing systems.* The existence of old or incompatible piping materials, as well as faulty fixtures and waste lines, are some of the most common problems with plumbing systems. Although potentially hazardous plumbing problems (such as leaky gas pipes) aren't all that common, many homes are indeed plagued by clogged drains, leaky pipes and toilets, and dripping faucets.

6. *Flawed exteriors.* Defects in a home's exterior, including windows, doors, and wall surfaces that let in water and drafts, are other common problems. Although they rarely cause structural troubles, they can cause discomfort and raise heating and cooling bills. Make sure your windows and doors have adequate caulking and weather-stripping.

7. *Poor ventilation.* While you don't want a drafty house, you also don't want to button up your home too tightly. Homes that are "oversealed"—and do not have adequate ventilation—retain excessive indoor moisture. This can lead to rot and mold. Install vents and fans in unvented bathrooms and cooking areas to prevent condensation from damaging plaster, wallboard, and windows.

8. *Poor overall maintenance.* Peeling paint, rotting decks, jammed garbage disposals, and broken light fixtures might seem more like cosmetic than serious problems, but they reflect the overall neglect of your home. Ignoring repairs does not make the need for them go away. "A prospective buyer is

leery of anything that raises a red flag," says Gladstone, "and the more red flags, the more skeptical he's going to be." Remember, every trouble spot that arouses the buyer's suspicions decreases the value of your home—by exactly how much depends on the scope of the problem and cost of labor and materials to fix it.

9. *Environmental problems.* These can include asbestos, formaldehyde, leaking underground oil tanks, contaminated drinking water, lead-based paint, and radon gas. These are important to address because, while they might not be visible to the eye, they can cause significant environmental damage and health consequences, particularly to children. (For more information about indoor air quality, asthma and allergies, mold and moisture, carbon monoxide, lead, drinking water, and pesticides, visit the Healthy Homes Web site at: *http://www.uwex.edu/healthyhome/topics.html.* The Healthy Homes Partnership is a collaboration of the U.S. Department of Agriculture and the Department of Housing and Urban Development. )

10. *Structural problems.* As a result of one or more problems in the previous categories, some homes might sustain damage to structural components such as foundation walls, floor joists, rafters, or window and door headers.

## A WORD ABOUT ROOF REPLACEMENT

Let's face it, roofs aren't sexy. It's just not as easy to get all worked up about new shingles as, say, an indoor spa with interior bench-style seating, 10 jets, and fingertip temperature control.

It's also a major expense. According to *Remodeling* magazine, the industry bible for remodeling professionals, the average roof replacement cost $11,399 in 2002. The resale value of that replacement is $7644. At an average return of 67 percent, roof replacement was one of the lowest-yielding investment returns of all the projects evaluated by *Remodeling* in 2002. (For a list of the top projects studied by the magazine in 2003 and how much money they recoup, see Chapter 3.)

So while it's absolutely necessary that you replace an antiquated and leaking roof, you might be rightfully reluctant to install a new one if the roof you have is aging but holding its own. After all, $11,000 goes a long way towards paying for that new spa.

| Roof Replacement | | | |
|---|---|---|---|
| **Market** | **Job Cost** | **Resale Value** | **Cost Recouped** |
| National average | $11,399 | $7,644 | 67 percent |

Source: *Remodeling* magazine, "2002 Cost vs. Value Report." Project description: Remove existing roofing to bare wood and dispose of properly. Install 30 squares of fiberglass asphalt shingles with new felt underlayment, galvanized drip edge, and mill-finish aluminum flashing.

These figures, however, can radically change in hot housing markets. According to *Remodeling,* the average roof replacement in Los Angeles in 2002 was priced at $13,392, but netted $18,370 just one year later—a phenomenal return of 137 percent. Variables, such as your regional housing market and what your neighbors are doing to improve their homes, should make you think twice before nixing that new roof.

In some cases, you can actually *double* your investment in a new roof, according to Gladstone, who is also president of Stonehollow Fine Home Inspections in Stamford, Connecticut.

Says Gladstone: "Let's say your house in perfect shape is worth $300,000. But it needs a new roof. For the sake of argument and round numbers, we'll say the new roof costs $5000. But you don't want to put in the extra expense. So you forget the roof and put your house on the market for $305,000. Then the buyer and the real estate agent come along. The home inspector tells them the roof is on its last legs and they automatically knock off $10,000 and only offer you $295,000.

Instead, you could spend the $5000 for the new roof, put the house on the market for $310,000, and you would most likely get it in a good market. The perception of the buyer is that a new roof has value. It's an expense and undertaking that he doesn't want to have to worry about."

Jim Cory, senior editor of *Remodeling,* agrees. "A well-maintained home has more value today than it did 20 years ago," he says. "People don't have the time today to invest in added repairs. They don't want the aggravation."

Like they say in those MasterCard® commercials: The cost of a new roof? Depending on the size of your home and where you live, anywhere from $5000 to $13,000. Freedom from repairs? Priceless. (Or darn close to it.)

# CHAPTER 3

# RECOUP YOUR REMODELING COSTS

# COST VERSUS VALUE

It's little wonder people look to their homes as a safe haven for their money, particularly when the stock market fluctuates wildly—and often in the wrong direction. But before you invest your hard-earned cash in remodeling projects to increase the value of your home, you need to have some idea of which projects are the equivalent of fool's gold (pretty to look at, but devoid of any real value) and which are worth their weight in gold.

But where do you begin?

We started with *Remodeling* magazine's annual "Cost vs. Value Report." The publication compares the estimated costs of popular home improvement projects, such as kitchen remodels and bathroom additions, with the value they're likely to add to your home. The costs for the projects are estimated by HomeTech Information Systems, a Bethesda, Maryland, company that publishes estimating software for professional remodelers. The resale value numbers are based on the professional judgment of members of the National Association of Realtors® (NAR). NAR surveys its member appraisers, sales agents, and brokers regarding the projects, collects the data, and tabulates the results. Another helpful feature is that the report gives project descriptions, price points, and value numbers for both midrange and upscale remodeling projects.

The report lists dollar figures for 35 metropolitan areas that are identified as top remodeling markets by the Joint Center for Housing Studies at Harvard University. Additionally, national averages are also given for each of the home improvement projects that are evaluated, and these are the figures we use in this book. (You can check out *Remodeling*'s annual "Cost vs. Value Report" on the Web at *http://www.remodeling.hw.net/*.)

Although we discuss each project individually in this book, below you'll find a comprehensive chart of some of the most popular remodeling projects in 2002 and 2003 and the cost vs. value for each.

**The Most Popular Remodeling Projects**

Note: All figures are national averages

| Job | Year | Job Cost | Resale Value | Cost Recouped |
|---|---|---|---|---|
| Deck Addition | 2003 | $6,304 | $6,661 | 104 percent |
| Siding Replacement | 2003 | $7,329 | $7,247 | 98 percent |
| Bathroom Addition, Midrange | 2003 | $15,519 | $15,418 | 95 percent |
| Two-Story Addition | 2002* | $69,857 | $65,524 | 94 percent |
| Bathroom Remodel, Upscale | 2003 | $23,544 | $21,627 | 92 percent |
| Bathroom Remodel, Midrange | 2003 | $10,088 | $9,107 | 90 percent |
| Bathroom Addition, Upscale | 2003 | $38,134 | $32,272 | 84 percent |
| Family Room Addition | 2003 | $53,983 | $43,931 | 81 percent |
| Major Kitchen Remodel, Upscale | 2003 | $68,962 | $56,711 | 80 percent |
| Basement Remodel | 2003 | $43,865 | $34,801 | 79 percent |
| Master Suite, Upscale | 2003 | $133,993 | $103,279 | 77 percent |
| Master Suite, Midrange | 2003 | $70,760 | $54,376 | 76 percent |
| Major Kitchen Remodel, Midrange | 2003 | $43,804 | $33,101 | 75 percent |
| Roof Replacement | 2002* | $11,399 | $7,644 | 67 percent |

Source: *Remodeling* magazine, 2002 and 2003, published by Hanley Wood.
(* This project was last evaluated by the magazine in 2002.)

Although the "Cost vs. Value" report is one of the industry's most detailed accounts of investment returns on popular home improvement projects, we urge you to remember that the cost and value figures are only *estimates*. They are dollar figures that are relative to specific neighborhoods. For example, if property values are stagnant or in decline in your neighborhood, a major remodeling project is unlikely to recoup much of its cost. However, if property values are skyrocketing in your neighborhood, the return could very well be higher than the report suggests. Additionally, resale prices can vary widely within neighborhoods and between individual streets and homes. Even if property values are rising all around you and you add a deck that turns out to be more of an eyesore than an oasis, then this home "improvement" can actually detract from your home's worth.

# A WORD ABOUT VARIABLES

Many factors influence the value of your home, so it helps to consider them when you're trying to figure out how much an improvement will cost and which projects will actually pay off the biggest dividends at resale. These variables include:

- *The cost of materials and labor.* Traditionally, the most expensive remodeling markets are those in which the home prices have dramatically escalated.

- *The asking price, actual selling price, and length of time on the market of homes in your neighborhood.* These three factors help determine the value of your home. They are the foundation of a real estate agent's "comparative market analysis," or CMA. A CMA helps you determine how to price your property if you want to sell it in one month, 90 days, six months, or a year. By comparing current market prices on properties similar to yours, properties that sold within a particular time frame, and properties that never sold, a real estate agent can tell you how long your home will need to stay on the market to get your asking price.

- *The types of homes and/or the features in those homes that are selling well.* If you live in a neighborhood of upscale executive ranches with three bathrooms each and your house is a cape with only one-and-a-half baths, you might have trouble recouping your home improvement investments–although adding another full bath might certainly help. If you're unfamiliar with the features of the homes in your neighborhood, you can get a good idea by attending some open houses in your area.

- *The kinds of remodeling projects completed by your neighbors.* During those open houses (or when chatting with your neighbors), ask lots of questions about what kinds of remodeling work your neighbors have done and whether they were do-it-yourself projects or professional remodels.

All these variables help you determine the value of your home. You can also find out what your neighbors' homes are worth by visiting your town hall. This information is public record, but depending on the town or city in which you live, it might be as simple as walking into the town assessor's office and asking for the information, or as hard and unpleasant as a do-it-yourself root canal. If you're really lucky, the information will be online.

Why not just rely on what you can eyeball during your walks around the neighborhood? Perhaps your neighbor has a 750-square-foot addition off the back of the house that you can't see from the road. Or perhaps they just added a $50,000 kitchen and remodeled the entire house. Often it is difficult to tell just by driving or walking by. And what do you do with this research? That's up to you. If you find that your home is below, or equal to, comparable homes in your neighborhood and town, you might decide to just plow ahead with your home improvement project. If your house is at the top end in your neighborhood, you might want to give it more thought. If you are planning to stay in your home forever, the fact that your home improvement project might overprice your house for your neighborhood is not a top concern.

At the same time, given today's rapidly changing job market where people are being moved around the country, you just might want to consider looking at larger homes, those that already have the type of addition you are contemplating. That doesn't mean you should move, but if you are concerned about how much money you will get out of your home when you eventually sell, moving is an option you should investigate. If you are really settled into your neighborhood, have great neighbors, and the kids have friends living two doors down, then perhaps putting down more permanent roots is the best decision for your family.

It's also helpful to speak with experienced contractors who work on these kinds of remodeling projects every day. For this book, we interviewed several 2003 Contractor of the Year (COTY) award winners. COTY awards are sponsored by The National Association of the Remodeling Industry, a not-for-profit trade association of the nation's remodelers. All COTY entries are judged on problem solving, functionality, aesthetics, craftsmanship, innovation, and the degree of difficulty of the project. (You'll find a list of these contractors and their award-winning projects in Chapter 14.)

# PART 2

# GET THE BIGGEST BIGGEST BANG FOR YOUR BUCK

# CHAPTER 4

# ADDITIONS: SIZE *DOES* MATTER (BUT FLOW IS MORE IMPORTANT)

# DO YOUR HOMEWORK

So you're thinking of taking the plunge and building onto your castle. Do you wonder what the experience will be like? Just tell a few family members, friends, coworkers, or neighbors that you're considering adding on. Then sit back. You'll soon hear all of the horror stories they have ever lived through—or heard about second or third hand.

You'll hear about the bathroom remodeling job that resulted in more leaking pipes, not less, the new master bedroom that doesn't have a wall large enough for the king-sized bed, and the $10,000 remodeling job that turned into a $30,000 boondoggle and took more than a year to complete.

Adding on doesn't have to be a nightmare, but it can easily become one if you don't do your homework. We spoke to many contractors and homeowners for this book. Every single one agreed with this simple fact: If you don't prepare well before the first shovel of dirt is turned, you're asking for trouble. Big trouble.

Lack of preparation increases the likelihood that your job will take longer than expected (sometimes much longer), multiplies the chances that your job will cost more than budgeted (sometimes *much* more), and will heighten the stress levels in your home. Don't underestimate the disruption in your life. If you have never done significant remodeling, you're in for a rude awakening. It's on par with the chaos of moving, but unlike a move, you can't just burn the midnight oil for a few days, unpack some boxes, and then get on with your life. It will go on for a couple of weeks. A couple of months. Maybe even a year.

OK, we've convinced you. You're willing to do your homework. But where do you start? Carl Seville, vice president of SawHorse Inc., an award-winning design-build firm in Atlanta, Georgia, says you

If you don't do your homework, you might just scare off some of the best remodelers in the business. For example, A.J. Paron-Wildes, general manager of Dreammaker Bath and Kitchen of St. Louis Park, Minnesota, says that people who wake up one morning and decide that "today is the day" (and that they need to remodel their home right now) concern her. Paron-Wildes, who also serves as a consultant for HGTV, says that it should take about two years from the initial project idea to completion. This ensures that you have thought everything through and that the end product will satisfy both your current and future needs.

should resist the temptation of trying to map out every minute detail of the home improvement process. Instead, he says, you're better off taking a step back and talking with your spouse and your children about what they would like to see improved in your home. Maybe you have a big family and you would like to host holiday gatherings, but you can't fit everyone in your dining room. Or perhaps your family is growing and each of your children wants his or her own bedroom and a quiet place where they can study. Or maybe there are five people in the house and only one bathroom and the math doesn't seem to be adding up first thing in the morning. Or the kids are driving you crazy and you and your spouse decide you need a space of your own—an oasis that not only includes a place to sleep, but also your own bathroom, and a closet that holds more than one season of clothes. (Now *that's* what we're talking about!)

Most people would love to have a bigger house. But you must sit down, prioritize your needs, and develop a plan of attack. Before you decide to add 3000 square feet of space onto your 1200-square-foot five-room ranch, you must speak with a real estate professional. Why? Because if you are the slightest bit concerned about getting a good return on your remodeling investment, you need to make sure that you aren't pricing yourself out of your neighborhood. (Review Chapter 3.) Remember, if you own one of the smaller homes on your street (or in your neighborhood) and it truly needs work, then you'll likely recoup more than if you own the largest home on your block and it's already in pristine condition.

Consumers are building additions today that are 20 to 30 percent larger than they did 20 years ago, says Alan Hanbury, treasurer of the award-winning House of Hanbury Builders in Newington, Connecticut. That's because people expect more from their homes today and have more disposable income. Also, folks are realizing that the cost per square foot actually *drops* as the size of the addition increases (all other things being equal).

According to Hanbury, the first 100 square feet might cost $200 per square foot, but by the time the addition increases to 300 square feet, the last square foot might be down to $75. The key to actually receiving that reduced per square foot price, is not adding "budget busters"—expensive items not in the original budget.

## GO WITH THE FLOW

From the outside, bad additions look like a helicopter dropped a box onto the side of your house. From the inside, bad additions make your house feel like a rabbit's warren.

"The key to any renovation is circulation," says Seville. Proper home design gives you the feeling that one room flows into the next, rather than a feeling that you're trapped inside a series of boxy, unconnected rooms.

Proper planning doesn't mean that your addition will cost more. It only means that it will likely work better for you and add more value to your home. "Open and airy is what they are looking for," says Sue Smith, a top-selling Prudential Connecticut Realty agent in Glastonbury,

Connecticut with 21 years of experience. For example, homes with kitchens that open into family rooms, allowing mothers to keep an eye on their children while preparing dinner are in great demand.

Good design is often rectangular, perhaps a family room 24-by-16 feet, taking into account that plywood and sheetrock comes in four-foot-wide sheets, so that you get the most return for your remodeling buck. Rectangular rooms look better from the outside and are much easier to decorate. Walk around your neighborhood and you can easily spot the bad additions: They look like they were slapped on. You'll have a more difficult time picking out houses that have well-designed additions because they seamlessly blend in with the original home.

One of the most difficult things for homeowners to do is to picture their completed additions. To give yourself a better visual, you can use grid paper to lay out your addition to scale. Home design software can help as well.

So you've done your homework and you've decided to go ahead and add on. Which projects give you the maximum return for your money? Four perennial favorites are:

- Two-story addition
- Bathroom addition
- Family room addition
- Master suite addition

## TWO-STORY ADDITION

Have you decided that your home needs a lot more space? Does the idea of transforming your space (not just simply remodeling it) excite you? Well then the two-story addition might just be the project for you. According to *Remodeling* magazine, the average two-story addition cost $69,857 in 2002. The resale value is $65,524, an average return of 94 percent.

| Two-story Addition | | | |
| --- | --- | --- | --- |
| Market | Job Cost | Resale Value | Cost Recouped |
| National average | $69,857 | $65,5240 | 94 percent |

Source: *Remodeling* magazine, "2002 Cost vs. Value Report." Project description: Add a 24-by-16 foot two-story wing over crawl space with a first-floor family room and a second-floor bedroom with full bath. Include 11 3-by-5-foot double-hung insulated windows; carpeted floors; painted drywall on walls and ceiling; and painted trim. In the family room, include a prefabricated gas fireplace and an atrium-style exterior door. In the 5-by-8-foot bathroom, include a one-piece fiberglass tub/shower unit; standard white toilet; wood vanity with ceramic tile countertop; resilient vinyl flooring; and mirrored medicine cabinet with built-in light strip, papered walls, and painted trim. Add new heating and cooling system to handle the addition.

Here is the best news about two-story additions: They cost less per square foot to build than two single-story additions. According to builder Alan Hanbury, a two-story addition can cost 30 percent less when compared to building two separate one-floor additions of the same square footage. That's because you only need to excavate once, you only need one roof, and if planned properly, you can line up plumbing and save a substantial amount of money.

The other good news is that you can use a variety of materials to cantilever the top floor so that the second story can be several feet larger than the first floor. This will provide you with additional design flexibility and help you add elements, such as a small deck overlooking the back yard. There is a downside to adding on, however. It is a complex job and you need to make sure that the people you hire can handle it.

Deciding to go ahead and build a two-story addition is a big step. It's going to cost you a substantial amount of money. That $69,524 could easily increase by 50 percent, 100 percent, or even 200 percent if you get carried away and start telling your contractor, "Well as long as your guys are here, you might as well . . ."

Once you start down this path, you can kiss your budget goodbye. For example, let's say that your addition hooks up to the kitchen on the bottom floor and access to the top floor is through an existing bedroom. The family room looks great and its style is modern. But your kitchen's design is so 1970s. So you decide to take the plunge and remodel it as well. (Peeking ahead into Chapter 5, you will see that the national average for remodeling a midrange kitchen is $43,804!) Or maybe you can live with the kitchen, but the bedroom through which you access the new master bedroom needs to be transformed into an office. And while you're adding the master bath, you really have the urge to gut the outdated upstairs bath. This way lies madness.

The key is to get a clear scope of the project, determine a budget, and resist the urge to expand the budget by huge multiples. That doesn't mean that you shouldn't consider the entire structure when taking on an extensive remodeling job. It just means that you should do so in the planning stages in order to minimize the amount and cost of any "surprises."

If you're planning a two-story addition, you must consider:

- The condition and age of the roof (especially if the new addition will tie into the existing structure). The average roof lasts about 20 years. However, if your roof is more than 10 years old, it should be inspected before you get started.
- Electrical needs. If you still have 60-amp service (and even if you have 100-amp service, but plan to add a substantial amount of load to your system), you might want to consider an upgrade to 200-amp service.
- Heating and air conditioning. Hire a qualified contractor to come in and do a heat loss analysis of your current system. The time to correct any problems is when the walls are open—not after the last picture is hung.

You need to stay particularly focused. You will have every type of contractor working on your two-story addition—the same as for anyone who is building a new house. That means you will likely spend several months under construction, perhaps six months or more. The good news is that two-story additions can actually be less disruptive to your home itself because you don't always have to open it up to the elements until the addition is well on its way to completion.

---

**TIPS FOR TWO-STORY ADDITIONS**

- *When building your master bedroom above the family room, add at least six inches of insulation in the ceiling of the family room. Why? Soundproofing. The last thing you want to hear is the latest Top 40 hit pulsating through the floor of your bedroom as you are trying to read a book or have a quiet conversation with your spouse.*
- *Add telephone and cable television jacks in your master bedroom. Don't forget that today's high-speed Internet access comes from a telephone jack or cable television wire, so be sure to add at least one jack of each to the spot in your bedroom where you might want a computer (unless you set up a wireless network in your home).*
- *Add external electrical plugs to your home if you like to illuminate your house for every holiday. While you're at it, put those plugs on wall switches so that you can turn them on and off from the comfort of your home.*

---

# BATHROOM ADDITION

We've come a long way since colonial times when family members took turns bathing once a week in a large tub in the kitchen. Even just 70 years ago, a three-bedroom house with one bath was common. Then about 40 years ago, an extra half bath snuck into the average home. Today, new homes are built with a bare minimum of two full baths and it's certainly not uncommon to see three or *more*.

If you're tired of waiting in line to get in the shower or you have high-maintenance teenagers who camp out in the bathroom for hours on end, maybe it's time that you carve out some space for another full bath. According to *Remodeling* magazine, the midrange cost of adding a full bath to your one or one-and-a-half bathroom home in 2003 was $15,519. The resale value of that remodel is $15,418, an excellent average return of 95 percent.

| Bathroom Addition (Midrange) | | | |
|---|---|---|---|
| Market | Job Cost | Resale Value | Cost Recouped |
| National average | $15,519 | $15,418 | 95 percent |

Source: *Remodeling* magazine, "2003 Cost vs. Value Report." Project description: Add a full 6-by-8-foot bath to a house with one or one and a half baths. Locate within existing footprint near bedrooms. Include cultured-marble vanity top, molded sink, standard tub/shower ceramic tile surround, low-profile toilet, general and spot lighting, mirrored medicine cabinet, linen storage, vinyl wallpaper, and ceramic tile floor.

Henry Ford once said you could choose any color Model T as long as it was black. In the 1940s, you could choose any color bathroom fixture, as long as it was white. The standard bath had a white cast iron tub, a white toilet, a white pedestal sink, and a white or white and black checked floor. Today, baths have been transformed. They aren't just rooms where you go to clean up, they are showpieces—no less decorated than any other room in the house.

If you have a very tight budget, you are going to have to choose elements for your new bathroom wisely. You can easily spend $65 for a toilet, or $365. You can shell out $199 for a tub, or $5000 for a top-of-the-line steam shower. You can pay $99 for a cultured marble vanity top, or 10 times that for polished granite. In fact, the average price of an upscale bathroom addition with a whirlpool tub was $38,134 in 2003, according to *Remodeling* magazine. Its resale value is $32,272, an average return of 84 percent.

| Bathroom Addition (Upscale) | | | |
| --- | --- | --- | --- |
| Market | Job Cost | Resale Value | Cost Recouped |
| National average | $38,134 | $32,272 | 84 percent |

Source: *Remodeling* magazine, "2003 Cost vs. Value Report." Project description: Add a new 9-by-9-foot master bath to an existing master bedroom. The new bathroom includes a 4-by-4-foot neo-angle shower with ceramic tile walls, recessed shower caddy, body spray fixture, and frameless enclosure as well as a personalized whirlpool tub; a solid surface countertop with two integral sinks, two mirrored medicine cabinets lighted by individual sconces, a compartmentalized commode area with one-piece toilet, and a humidistat-controlled exhaust fixture. Other touches: heated floor and towel bars, custom drawer base, and wall cabinets.

Everyone has a different vision of what the ideal bathroom should look like. But there are universal elements you must consider when outfitting one. They are:

- **Tile.** Most folks want a ceramic tile floor because it looks solid, is easy to maintain, and is durable. That's the easy part. The hard part is finding the exact tile for your bathroom floor. Finding the right color tile is even more difficult than finding the right color of paint from one of those massive paint chip displays in your local home improvement store.

  You must also make sure that the tile in your new bath is set properly. If not, grout can loosen and mold can invade your home, something you should avoid at all costs. According to bath designer A.J. Paron-Wildes "when you get married you spend money on a good photographer" so when you build a bathroom addition, you should always "spend money on a good tile setter."

  If you decide to have a tile tub surround, be sure you install cement board behind it. That's because not having a rigid base on which to put the tile in moist areas can lead to loose tiles and moisture problems. Mold in your walls can be a very expensive problem to fix.

> **TIP:** *Color choices can be overwhelming, but if you are concerned with resale value, you should consider neutral colors. Why? Remember those orange countertops in the 1960s? Or how about the gold kitchen appliances of the 1970s? Sure, that purple tub might be the epitome of designer fashion today, but do you think it will still be in style in 5 or 10 years? This doesn't mean you should always stick with white to be on the safe side, but you should stay away from extreme colors or jarring color combinations*

- **Toilet.** Most homeowners today install low-profile toilets that make the average-sized bathroom feel a bit larger. But you might not be able to go the home improvement store and just pick out any model that you like. That's because in many parts of the country, low-flow toilets are mandated as water conservation measures.

  (Even if your area doesn't mandate them, you might want to consider them and, in turn, spend less money on water—or use less of your well—and save the environment at the same time.)

  Low-flow toilets are not created equal. Talk with someone who went the low-end route with a water-saver toilet. Chances are good they'll have a few things to tell you about trying (and failing) to keep them clean.

- **Tub.** Tubs are made of fiberglass (the least expensive and least durable), cast iron (the heaviest), and acrylic (generally regarded as having the most durable finish).

  There are pros and cons for each and there is no simple answer as to which one is best for every circumstance. While a fiberglass tub is the least durable, if the bathroom is only lightly used, then it probably will meet your needs—as long as you install it properly. (Make sure it is supported from the bottom.)

  Cast iron tubs will provide you with more durability than fiberglass and some say they have a sturdier look and feel to them. Acrylic tubs are the hardiest because the color is solid throughout the material. If your bath will be heavily used, you should stick with the cast iron or acrylic models.

- **Vanity/sink**. The two main options for washing up in your new bathroom are a pedestal sink and a sink set into a vanity. Everything else being equal, you should consider storage in your investment and resale equation because folks always want as much storage as possible. That doesn't mean you must automatically rule out a pedestal sink. Instead, match it up with an oversized medicine cabinet, a large linen closet, or perhaps even another storage cabinet in the bathroom.

  If you decide on a traditional vanity, remember that the cabinet portion is really a piece of furniture and should be treated as such. Think practicality here—drawers versus doors—and which option best suits your family's needs. As for the vanity top, cultured marble is the most cost-effective, but more expensive manmade materials such as Corian®, as well as natural materials such as granite or quartz, give a solid appearance and are extremely durable.

If you're on a tight budget, you will also have to apply discipline when it comes to choosing bathroom accessories. Here again, the options are nearly limitless. Some of the most popular include:

- **Heated floor**. Twenty years ago, it seemed as if everyone wanted a heat lamp in the bathroom. But today, particularly in northern climates, more people are clamoring for heated floors. There are two ways to heat a floor, either with piped water or electrical wires beneath the tile. The electrical method is by far the less expensive route, but it can still add $1000 to the cost of a tile floor.

  Heated bathroom floors eliminate the biggest complaint about tile floors—that they're cold on your feet. With a wall-mounted thermostat, you can select the degree of warmth.

While electric heat is notoriously expensive for heating an entire home, heated bathroom floors only cost about $1 per week in electricity.

- **Faucet.** You can get faucets for $40 or $400. And while you might want to spend a little more for the washerless designs, unless you are building a high-end bathroom, you might want to put your money elsewhere. Remember, because you probably want your sink and bath faucets to complement each other, your $400 could quickly turn into $800!

  Concerned about resale value when it comes to faucet finishes? Well, brass is out and nickel is in, so you know what that means: A stainless steel faucet is pretty much timeless.

- **Bathroom fan.** Next to floors, a bathroom fan will be your most important purchase. Why? Because if you don't install one, or you install one that is too small, your investment will be on its way to becoming a detriment to the value of your home, rather than an asset. Have you ever stepped into the tropical rainforest that is a bathroom after any two teenagers in a row have showered in there? Then you know exactly what we're talking about. The fastest way to reduce the value of your bath is to allow excessive moisture to remain in your bathroom, causing the walls to drip, the cabinets to warp, and the fixtures to pit.

---

**TIP:** *Bathroom fans are rated in cubic feet per minute. Measure the size of your bathroom, then buy a fan for a room that is 50 to 100 percent larger than yours. This might be the best investment that you ever make for your bathroom. With proper maintenance, the fan will keep your bathroom looking like new for years to come.*

---

# FAMILY ROOM ADDITIONS

Family rooms have also undergone a dramatic transformation. Twenty years ago, the living room was more formal and the family room was a casual place where the family plunked down on the old couch to watch TV.

Today, family rooms take on four basic forms:

1. *Traditional family rooms* that resemble any other room in the house, only bigger.

2. *Sunrooms* that include a lot of windows that appear to bring the outdoors inside.

3. *Media rooms*, where windows are minimal so that you can enjoy glare-free viewing of your plasma television and flat-panel computer monitor.

4. *Any combination of the above.*

When they have the choice, consumers most often opt to have their family room attached to the kitchen, says David Adams of David Adams Design in Sandy Hook, Connecticut. This creates a large, open meeting area. Parents want to be able to watch the children playing while they converse with family and friends who've come to visit. In 2003, the national average cost for a 16-by-25-foot family room was

| Family Room Addition | | | |
|---|---|---|---|
| Market | Job Cost | Resale Value | Cost Recouped |
| National average | $53,983 | $43,931 | 81 percent |

Source: *Remodeling* magazine, "2003 Cost vs. Value Report." Project description: In a style and location appropriate to the existing house, add a 16-by-25-foot room on a crawl space foundation with wood siding and a fiberglass shingle roof. Include drywall interior with batt insulation, prefinished hardwood floor, and 10 square feet of glazing including windows, atrium-style exterior doors, and two operable skylights. Tie into existing heating and cooling.

$53,983, according to *Remodeling* magazine. The resale value of that addition is $43,931, a return of 81 percent.

To squeeze out the largest return from a family room addition, you might want to err on the side of brighter, while minimizing the number and size (consider none) of windows on the west side. That's because the sun sets in the west and can add unwelcome amounts of heat and glare to your room. Brighter is better for resale value, because even if a prospective buyer wants a media room, they can always add room-darkening shades or drapes. It is much more difficult (and costly) to add natural light to a room. As for room sizes, Adams says that rectangular-sized additions tend to blend in with the existing structure better, so they are preferred.

Below are several questions to ask yourself to help decide which type of family room will best suit your needs:

- How will the use of this family room differ from the living room?
- How big is my family?
- Do we want a large sitting area?
- Do we prefer a media room with less glass or a sunroom with more glass?
- What will be the room's focal point? A large window? A fireplace? Built-ins? Or a large-screen TV?

As you contemplate both the functionality and resale value of your new family room, also consider these "must haves" for your addition:

- A spot for a large (40 to 50 inch) television. Today you can buy a television the size of a couch. You need a spot for a television that size—even if you don't yet own one quite that big.
- Make sure you are wired for various media. That means you need at least one cable hookup in the room and at least one

telephone jack. Even if you don't plan on having high-speed Internet access in your family room, you might change your mind later on.

- Consider incorporating a spot in your new room for the family computer. Many parents today only want Internet access where they can monitor it. What better place than the family room?

- If the room is large enough, think about having a separate section where kids can play. It will make it easier to enjoy adult conversation in your new room.

- Storage, storage, and more storage. There might come a day when you'll say your house is too big for your needs, but we've yet to meet the person who says he or she has too much storage space. When shopping for a new home, buyers always look for lots of places to store their accumulated "stuff." Sneaking in built-in cabinets and perhaps a closet or two can only increase the value of your home.

- Flexible lighting. This means the room is designed for a variety of overhead and table lighting to create different moods. You need to rely on a combination of ceiling and table lighting to provide proper illumination.

- In most parts of the country, a gas fireplace is a must-have in the family room. Modern gas fireplaces are a far cry from those old electric fireplaces sold 30 years ago that consisted of a light bulb and a piece of colored plastic rotating in front of it. Today, gas fireplaces (in either natural gas or propane) offer realistic orange-colored flames, with "burning embers," brick inserts, and ceramic glass.

  Some models are so powerful, they are rated as gas furnaces. These come with remote controls that not only turn the flames on and off, but also with thermostats that keep the room at a constant temperature. Some models come with blowers and optional ductwork to send some of that heat to other rooms. This can save you money when it comes time to add heat to a room that is quite a distance from the furnace. You can use the fireplace as a sole source of warmth for the room. They are also cleaner to use than woodstoves, quite important if anyone in your family has asthma or other respiratory problems that are aggravated by wood smoke.

# ADDING A MASTER SUITE

How would you describe a master suite? An oasis? A retreat? An escape?

Today's master suites are all of these, resembling efficiency apartments that not only come complete with their own bathrooms, but with their own televisions, sitting areas, dressing rooms—even wine refrigerators, coffeemakers, and microwaves, too. A master suite was once a place where you went to get away for a couple of hours. Today you can go in after work on Friday and not emerge until Monday morning!

According to *Remodeling* magazine, the national average for a midrange master suite cost $70,760 in 2003. The resale value is $54,376, an average return of 76 percent.

But today's homeowners aren't looking for a simple master bedroom in the shape of a box. They're looking for a bright room with plenty of space for traditional bedroom furniture. They want

**Master Suite, Midrange**

| Market | Job Cost | Resale Value | Cost Recouped |
|---|---|---|---|
| National average | $70,760 | $54,376 | 76 percent |

Source: *Remodeling* magazine, "2003 Cost vs. Value Report." Project description: On a house with two or three bedrooms, add a 24-by-16-foot master bedroom suite over a crawl space. Include walk-in closet/dressing area, whirlpool tub in ceramic tile platform, separate 3-by-4-foot ceramic tile shower, and double-bowl vanity with solid surface countertop. Bedroom floor is carpet; bath floor is ceramic tile. Painted walls, ceiling, and trim. General and spot lighting, exhaust fan.

nooks and crannies where they can place comfortable reading chairs, tables, and perhaps a bookcase and computer desk. Living rooms are no longer the sole domain of fireplaces. Increasingly, gas fireplaces are turning up in bedrooms, adding to the ambiance of the room. Luxurious larger master baths/suites can also include room for a wine refrigerator, coffeemaker, and microwave. And don't forget the linen closet. If you don't have one in the main house, a linen closet in your master suite can free up your master closet for clothes and shoes storage only.

However, if you are planning this kind of high-end dramatic retreat, you can easily wind up spending twice the national average cost of a master suite addition. Throw in that gas fireplace with stone hearth and custom mantle and a hospitality center/kitchenette and you could easily end up topping $133,993, the average price tag for an upscale master suite in 2003, according to *Remodeling* magazine. The resale value of this project is $103,279, a return of 77 percent on your original investment.

The most costly part of your master suite will be your master bath, an area in which you can quickly blow your budget. A word of caution here: If your contractor provides an allowance for the master bath, be sure to do your shopping for fixtures and accessories before signing the contract. You want to make sure that the allowance he

| Master Suite, Upscale | | | |
|---|---|---|---|
| Market | Job Cost | Resale Value | Cost Recouped |
| National average | $133,993 | $103,279 | 77 percent |

Source: *Remodeling* magazine, "2003 Cost vs. Value Report." Project description: Add a 24-by-16-foot master suite with sleeping and sitting areas adjacent to large master bath. Include custom bookcases, woodworking details, and built-in storage; high-end gas fireplace with stone hearth and custom mantle; and large walk-in closet/dressing area. Add French doors accessing outdoor space. Bath includes large walk-in shower, stone shower walls and floor, and a frameless glass enclosure. Add whirlpool tub into stone platform with cabinet front. Include two vanities with stone countertops and large mirrors. Add hospitality center/kitchenette. Include soundproofing, in-floor heating, custom wall finishes and hardware, general and spot lighting, and lighting controls.

provides is sufficient to cover the quality of the items that you pick out. Sometimes the contractor's allowance is much too low. Or you might tell him that you want a basic bathroom and then change your mind as you begin shopping and see all of the options available.

Although whirlpool tubs have been extremely popular in the last few years, they are quickly going out of style for four basic reasons:

- Many people simply don't have the time to use them.
- Unless you have a large water heater, these big tubs can leave you sitting in lukewarm bathwater.
- You're not supposed to use bath oils or bubble bath in whirlpool tubs because bacteria can accumulate in the jets.
- Big tubs leave little room leftover for shower stalls and most folks prefer a daily shower to a bath.

Today, homeowners are choosing to install bubble-type tubs in which you can use aromatherapy bath oils and bubble bath. And while you might see pictures of bathrooms in design magazines with steps leading up to the tub, many contractors will advise you against them. When ceramic tile gets wet, it is slippery and dangerous.

Along with the bubble tubs come stall showers of at least 36 inches square. Higher-end options in showers today include steam showers, in which the door is sealed and tile runs floor to ceiling and multiple-head showers with room enough for two. Also popular are benches in showers so that women can sit down to shave their legs and large-head showers up to 12 to 18 inches across that soak your entire body at once. According to builder Alan Hanbury, homeowners also want clear glass shower doors that make the room look bigger and sexier. And when it comes to vanities in the master bath, double bowls are standard these days so that a couple can get ready to go out or go to work at the same time.

Tile, often hand-painted, is also quite popular on the floors and walls of today's master baths. As for tile sizes, bath designer A.J. Paron-Wildes says a common mistake is to shy away from large-sized tiles. Using large tile on the floor (12-by-12 or even 18-by-18 inch), can actually make the room appear larger, she says. One advantage of using larger tile means that you will have fewer lines, providing a less cluttered feel to the room. Consider setting the tile diagonally. It will cost you about 10 percent more, but it will also make the room appear larger than it actually is. This little tip can help boost the return on your investment at resale because homebuyers want that spacious look throughout their homes.

## A WORD ABOUT MASTER CLOSETS

Master bedroom closets are usually the largest in the home and so they're asked to take on many jobs. Not only are they required to hold four seasons of clothes for two people, but they are often used for blanket and suitcase storage and for hiding gifts, as well. Today, women especially are asking for larger master closets that also include storage for undergarments and a place to sit where they can dress. Builder David Adams says that couples want closets as large as possible and, whenever he can, he adds both "his and hers" master closets. Building them at least six feet wide allows for substantial storage on both sides.

While closets formerly consisted of a rod or two for hanging clothes and perhaps a couple of shelves for shoe storage, today entire closet organizer systems costing hundreds of dollars are common. Many add additional shelving and even drawers to store even more clothing and accessories.

# CHAPTER 5

# INTERIOR IMPROVEMENTS: CABINETS, COUNTERTOPS, AND STATUS SYMBOLS, OH MY!

# KITCHEN REMODEL

Do your guests always drift into your kitchen from your perfectly pleasant living room and wind up conversing around your kitchen table? Join the club. Ever since people first brought fire indoors, the "hearth" has remained the heart of a home. It's also your home's busy nerve center where a variety of activities take place, including food preparation, cooking, homework, bill paying—even arts and crafts and sewing. So it's little wonder the kitchen is the most frequently remodeled room and the first place a potential buyer looks to determine whether a home has been consistently cared for.

The kitchen is also one room where you can add a lot of value to your home through improvements. According to *Remodeling* magazine, the average midrange kitchen remodel costs $43,804. The resale value of that remodel is $33,101, an average return of 75 percent. That number improves dramatically when you ramp up the project to include cherry cabinets and the latest built-in appliances, says Jim Cory, the magazine's senior editor.

According to Cory, the average top-of-the-line kitchen remodel costs $68,962, but recoups $56,711, an excellent return of 80 percent. The return is much better for the upscale kitchen because high-end features such as granite countertops and hardwood cabinets are now considered "must-haves" in upper-tier homes.

People remodel their homes for all kinds of reasons: to increase value, to add more space, and to improve traffic flow. But when it comes to *kitchens*, there is another reason why many folks remodel: to impress their parents, friends, and neighbors.

"Kitchens are status symbols," says Cory. For example, he tells of a contractor who built a brand-new $80,000 kitchen for a client about

| Kitchen Remodel (Midrange) | | | |
|---|---|---|---|
| Market | Job Cost | Resale Value | Cost Recouped |
| National average | $43,804 | $33,101 | 75 percent |

Source: *Remodeling* magazine, "2003 Cost vs. Value Report." Project description: Update 200-square-foot kitchen with 30 linear feet of semicustom grade wood cabinets, including a 3-by-5-foot island, and laminate countertops, standard double-tub stainless-steel sink with single-lever faucet. Also include energy efficient wall oven, cooktop, ventilation system, built-in microwave, dishwasher, garbage disposal, and custom lighting. Add new resilient floor. Paint walls, trim, and ceiling.

three years ago. "She called him recently to make sure he'd hooked up her gas oven to the [gas] line. Now what does that tell you? That she was willing to spend a lot of money on a state-of-the-art gas oven that she has never even used."

Let's face it, although the kitchen is one of the very first rooms that people see when they enter a home, and it's where many of us congregate throughout the day, most of us don't have wads of cash to remodel one—and then never use it. This is one room in which the budget reigns especially supreme.

"The kitchen is one room where you have to compromise all the way through or you can end up spending $60,000 pretty quickly," says Steve Hendy, an owner of Neal's Construction Co. in Cincinnati, Ohio. Bob Clements, owner of Bath & Kitchen Creations in Fairfax,

| Kitchen Remodel (Upscale) | | | |
|---|---|---|---|
| Market | Job Cost | Resale Value | Cost Recouped |
| National average | $68,962 | $56,711 | 80 percent |

Source: *Remodeling* magazine, "2003 Cost vs. Value Report." Project description: Update 200-square-foot kitchen with 30 linear feet of custom cherry cabinets, stone countertops, and imported ceramic tile backsplash. Also include built-in refrigerator, cooktop, 36-inch commercial grade range and vent hood, built-in warming drawer, trash compactor, built-in combination microwave and convection oven, high-end undermount sink and designer faucets, and built-in water filtration system. Add task lighting, including low-voltage undercabinet lights. Install cork flooring and cherry trim.

Virginia, agrees. "You have to deal with the budget issue upfront and there's always a degree of sticker shock."

However, there are ways to compromise that will still add value to your home, Clements says. One of his favorite tricks is to put less expensive laminate on the kitchen counters, but trim the edges with wood that matches the kitchen cabinets. "It's a $300 upgrade, but it looks much more expensive than that," he says.

---

**Kitchen Sticker Shock, 1850s-style:** Although it was unseemly to covet status symbols in the 1850s, many a housewife had her eye on the latest in cooking technology: the woodstove. These marvels consumed much less wood than a hearth, but the new technology didn't come cheap. The average price of a new woodstove in the 1850s was approximately $14. One dollar in 1850 is worth the equivalent of $22.02 today, according to the U.S. Department of Labor.

---

# FIVE IMPROVEMENTS THAT DRAMATICALLY TRANSFORM YOUR KITCHEN

Painting is obviously one of the least expensive and most dramatic ways to update your kitchen, but don't just start and stop there. First, assess the current state of the room. Is there enough storage space? Are your cabinets nicked? Are there any burn marks on your countertops? Is your kitchen (and its contents) more than 10 years old? (If so, it's definitely outdated—no matter how pristine the condition.)

In your kitchen, you get the biggest bang for your remodeling buck by addressing the problems mentioned above. To increase the value of your home, perform these five kitchen improvement projects:

1. *Install new cabinets*: Cabinets are a prime visual focal point in any kitchen They're also by far the biggest percentage of cost in most kitchen remodels—as much as 70 percent of your whole budget. While hardwood cabinets are the most durable and of the highest quality, they are also the most expensive. Typical high-quality cabinetry in a 10-foot-by-12-foot kitchen can cost upwards of $40,000.

   If custom cherry cabinets are out of your price range, consider cabinets constructed from manmade materials, such as pressboard or particleboard, but faced with real hardwood doors. These cabinets fall into the $7000 to $15,000 price range. Use caution, though, when selecting these. Particleboard often cannot withstand the weight of heavy canned goods over time and there are often drawer-glide problems and warping.

   Repainting your cabinets can also save you lots of money, but it doesn't make sense to do so if your cabinets are falling apart, says builder Steve Hendy. "It's like putting a new paint job on a car that doesn't run," he says. If your cabinets are in shabby shape, try to save money elsewhere and get the best-quality cabinets you can afford.

2. *Install new countertops*: Nothing improves your kitchen's look and feel (hence its value) quite like new countertops. Today, countertops are made from a dizzying array of materials, including laminate (such as Formica®), an amazing variety of domestic and imported tile, Corian® (a solid surfacing brand made by DuPont that can be cut, routed, drilled, sculpted, bent, or worked like wood), and polished stone, such as quartz and granite.

   Do-it-yourselfers and contractors use them all, but granite is definitely in big demand right now. According to Tony Paulos, president of award-winning Block Builders of Bethesda, Maryland, granite countertops "set the tone for the kitchen and the rest of the home" and say "quality" in a way that the others (particularly the laminates) do not.

Granite countertops for an average 18-by-20-foot kitchen (including an island) cost about $5000 and are definitely on the high end of the expense spectrum, followed by Corian®. Although Corian® has several different price points, the high-end products are nearly as expensive as granite, so many kitchen designers advise their clients to go with the granite instead.

This trend has not gone unnoticed or unchallenged by DuPont. The company has produced a white paper comparing Corian® and granite. You can read it at *http://www.corian.com/CorianPublic/corian/documents/pdf/co randgran.pdf*. The main difference between Corian® and granite, besides price, is that granite only comes in a handful of colors and is porous (allows liquid to seep in), so a surface sealer must be applied and maintained. Corian® is nonporous (impermeable to liquid) and comes in more than 90 colors. While it is true that a hot pot will leave scorch marks on Corian®, it is also true that a hot pot will damage granite's sealant coat and, over time, might discolor the stone. In either case, trivets or heat-resistant tile (which can be strategically set right into the countertop) will solve this problem.

---

**TIPS:** *What if you can't afford to install all-granite countertops? An excellent compromise is to save money by only using granite on an island and remodeling the other countertops in laminate or tile. There's no rule that says you have to do all your countertops the same. Mix and match is quite acceptable—and downright fashionable—if done well.*

*Additionally, don't overlook accessories that buyers don't necessarily think of themselves, but function as nice selling points at resale. Soap dispensers built right into countertops and sinks with built-in dish dividers are extra little touches that indicate quality.*

---

3. *Replace outdated appliances:* Besides the knotty pine cabinets, nothing dates your kitchen quite like a harvest gold gas range with four burners on top and a two-rack oven below. Now is the time to look into updating your stove, refrigerator, and dishwasher—and perhaps adding a trash compactor if you don't already have one.

Because technology changes so fast, chances are good that if you haven't shopped for appliances in awhile, you will be amazed. Appliances now have so many features, gadgets, and gizmos that you might feel you need a license to use them. Want to bake chocolate chip cookies in four minutes? No problem. Investigate buying a fast-cook oven that uses halogen lights and microwaves to cook a whole roasted chicken in less time than it takes to walk your dog four blocks and back. GE's Advantium models cost anywhere between $749 and $1,999 and are designed to fit above most cooktops, ranges, or countertops. The built-in wall oven can be installed either above a conventional single wall oven, above a warming drawer, or by itself.

Subzero wine chillers, with temperature settings for red and white wines, Viking and Bosch cooktops and ranges, and whisper-quiet Miele dishwashers—what contractor Tony Paulos calls the "Mercedes Package"—are on most home-owners' ultimate wish lists. Yet these amenities, together with a state-of-the-art stainless steel cook hood, can cost you upwards of a budget-busting $52,000.

Don't despair. It is perfectly possible to update your entire kitchen with good-quality brand-name appliances such as GE, Kenmore, Kitchen Aid, and Amana for $5000 to $8000. However, Paulos says his remodeling clients "in the know" still prefer European-made dishwashers because the most popular models are virtually silent.

**What is a "resilient" floor?** Resilient floors have some "give" to them and are mostly used in kitchens and baths. Some people refer to resilient floors incorrectly as linoleum. Linoleum is a natural product composed of linseed oil, cork, limestone, and wood resins while the most common resilient floor covering is sheet vinyl and vinyl composition tiles, or VCT. Other resilient floors include rubber and cork.

4. *Install new flooring:* You don't have to break the bank to put in a new floor that will have a huge impact on the overall appeal of your new kitchen. The choices are nearly limitless, but each type of flooring has its pros and cons. (See "A Word about Flooring" at the end of this section.)

   When shopping for flooring, you must consider your lifestyle as well as your budget. Do you have young children? You don't want your toddler falling on hard ceramic tile. Will there be dogs running through your kitchen on the way to their water bowls? Then you don't want flooring that will show scratches, such as wood. You must also consider the environment right outside your kitchen door. Is there a patio with gravel? Then think twice about installing vinyl that is susceptible to "ground-in" bits of dirt and tiny stones — unless you can train your kids to wipe their feet before and after they enter the kitchen.

   Another popular choice for kitchen flooring is laminate, which is similar in construction to Formica® countertops. Laminate flooring is a tongue-and-groove interlocking flooring system that comes in either planks or squares made of layers of resin, wood fiber, or paper bonded together for strength. The

> **TIP:** *Do you want the designer look of imported ceramic tile but your budget and your lifestyle dictate otherwise? Don't sweat it. Install a durable, less expensive option (such as vinyl composition or laminate tiles) for a look that mimics ceramic tile. You can always replace the "faux" stuff with the real deal in a few years when your kids are older and you have more financial resources.*

flooring has both a decorative layer (a print of a photograph of real wood, marble, granite, or ceramic) and a wear layer, which is applied to the decorative print layer to protect the pattern.

5. *Update your lighting:* Today's multitasking kitchens demand versatile lighting. Gone are the days when a single 100-watt fixture centered in the kitchen's ceiling was sufficient. "I see people every day who are saddled with one light in the middle of the kitchen," says Geoff Dent, president of Dent Electrical Supply in Danbury, Connecticut. "This means that everywhere around the perimeter, where most of the work is done, is done in one's own shadow."

According to Dent, the right recipe for lighting your kitchen depends on the size and complexity of the room. Small kitchens might require only a central ceiling fixture and task lighting tucked under a cabinet. More elaborate kitchens will demand a blend of general, task, and accent lighting. The good news is that lighting is a relatively small portion of your kitchen remodeling budget, but it has the potential to deliver dramatic results that add value to your home.

# BATHROOM REMODEL

A remodeled bathroom or bathroom addition has the most potential to increase the value of your home of all the interior home improve-

---

**TIPS: FIVE WAYS TO LIGHT UP YOUR KITCHEN**

1. *Time for recess:* For even illumination, install recessed lights over the stove and sink to create adequate task lighting for cooking and cleaning.

2. *Powerful pendant:* Kitchen tables and islands are natural focal points. A decorative pendant light with a dimmer switch combines function with dramatic flair.

3. *Under and over:* Use minitrack lights over and under cabinets to light up countertops and accent ceilings.

4. *Mix it up:* Wire the lights separately to create "zones." This lets you "layer" the light by using zones in different combinations.

5. *Bulbilicious:* Use the same color bulbs throughout your kitchen so that the tone of your floor, counters, and cabinets will all look the same. Halogen bulbs offer a whiter, more accentuating light that makes people and food look better.

Source: American Lighting Association

---

ments. This is because today's bathroom doubles as a sanctuary, a place where you can go at end of a long, hard day to escape the kids, forget about work, get clean, and relax. When buyers come calling at resale, they will especially delight in a bathroom that not only is good-looking and functional, but also captures their imagination. What gets

---

**Bathroom Remodel (Midrange)**

| Market | Job Cost | Resale Value | Cost Recouped |
|---|---|---|---|
| National average | $10,088 | $9,107 | 90 percent |

Source: *Remodeling* magazine, "2003 Cost vs. Value Report." Project description: Update an existing bathroom that is at least 25 years old. Replace all fixtures to include standard-size tub with ceramic tile surround, toilet, solid-surface vanity counter with integral double sink, recessed medicine cabinet, ceramic tile floor, vinyl wallpaper.

---

a buyer's attention? It might be as small as a built-in and lighted cosmetic/shaving mirror or as grand as a granite pedestal sink with sleek gold-plated faucets.

Just because your bathrooms are the smallest rooms in your home, don't assume a bathroom remodel is going to be cheap—especially if you are going to enlarge an existing bathroom. Unless you are doing the work yourself, remodeling a bathroom is so expensive because the work involves *all* the trades and you can't squeeze in more than one person at a time to do the work. "The bathroom is the part of the house with the densest assortment of materials and finishes," says Dan Blitzer of the American Lighting Association. "You have wall tile, floor tile, shower tile, faucet hardware, towel bars, wallpaper, and paint all in a space often smaller than 100 square feet."

According to *Remodeling* magazine, the average midrange bathroom remodel costs $10,088. The resale value of that remodel is $9107, an average return of 90 percent. The average top-of-the-line bathroom remodel costs $23,544, but recoups $21,627, a terrific return of 92 percent.

---

**Bathroom Remodel (Upscale)**

| Market | Job Cost | Resale Value | Cost Recouped |
|---|---|---|---|
| National average | $23,544 | $21,627 | 92 percent |

Source: *Remodeling* magazine, "2003 Cost vs. Value Report." Project description: Expand an existing 5-by-7-foot bathroom to 9-by-9 feet within existing house footprint. Include 30 square feet of windows and/or skylights. Relocate and replace tub with custom 4-by-6-foot shower with top-of-the-line fittings and full-body wash shower wall, tile enclosure, and glass block surround. Relocate the toilet into a partitioned area and replace it with one-piece color unit. Add bidet, stone countertops in custom vanity cabinet with twin designer sinks, and a linen/towel storage closet. Add tile floor, papered walls, and hardwood trim. Add general and spot lighting and a humidstat-controlled exhaust fan.

# FIVE IMPROVEMENTS THAT DRAMATICALLY TRANSFORM YOUR BATHROOM

Whether you're contemplating a midrange or upscale bathroom remodel, perform these five bathroom improvements to increase the overall value of your home:

1. *Install new countertops*: As in the kitchen, your bathroom countertops set the tone for the rest of the room. When choosing materials, you must consider style and function. Also, carefully consider maintenance.

   Granite countertops are as popular in today's bathrooms as they are in kitchens, but highly polished granite can scratch. Limestone, slate, and marble look gorgeous, but they are also very porous and must be sealed every six months— not a good choice for high traffic/kid-friendly bathrooms. A solid surface material such as Corian® might be better in these types of bathrooms because nicks and scratches can be sanded out and the sink can be integrated seamlessly. However, staining is sometimes a problem.

2. *Replace the sink and faucet*: This can be done as inexpensively or as pricey as you want. Manufacturers (such as Delta®, Moen®, Kohler®, and others) produce many styles, colors, and finishes to choose from. At the Delta® Web site, you can even build your own faucet at *http://www.deltafaucet.com/oncat/byof.html*.

---

**TIP:** *Never have enough shelf space in your bathroom? A neat trick is to extend the bathroom vanity with an arm that continues the vanity top over the toilet to create a little ledge.*

---

Match the style of your new faucet to new bathroom accessories, such as towel bars and drawer pulls.

3. *Install a new shower and/or tub*: The centerpiece of any full bath is the shower or tub—or combination of the two. It's here that personal preference dictates how you'd like to get clean—either by long, luxurious soaks, quick pulsating showers, or something in between the two. It's also here where you can opt to streamline your budget and get the no-frills white enamel bathtub for $200 or splurge for something like the 41-inch-by-75-inch Kohler sok™ (pronounced "soak"), an overflowing air bath with chromatherapy. For somewhere in the neighborhod of $7000, you can float chin-deep in a warm cocoon of water that continuously spills over the tub's rim into a water channel and is reheated and recirculated while special air jets create tiny soothing bubbles. The tub also features four underwater LED light ports that move gradually through a progression of eight colors. If you find a color you like, a touch of a button will hold that color indefinitely.

Although the sok™ might be a bit too high-tech or expensive for many homeowners' needs, air baths are definitely gaining in popularity over whirlpools, according to remodeling contractors. For one thing, air jets create lots of tiny bubbles while water jets blast just a few parts of your body. You can also use bubble bath or aromatherapy salts in an air bath and not worry about clogging the jets or causing a buildup of bacteria. Air baths also tend to be quieter than many whirlpools.

Despite the rising popularity of air baths, however, statistics show that the majority of homeowners (69 percent) actually prefer to shower rather than take a bath. Bob Clements, owner of Bath and Kitchen Creations in Fairfax, Virginia, is not surprised. "We live in a very fast-paced society," he says. "If you have a whirlpool, you have to wait for the water to warm

Bath or shower? Even if time were not an issue, the majority of Americans would still prefer to shower rather than take
a bath. In 2000, a nationwide survey of adults revealed that
69 percent of us prefer a shower, while just 29 percent would
rather take a bath.

There was a sharp contrast between the genders.
Overwhelmingly, 81 percent of men prefer to shower and
only 18 percent would take a bath if time allotted. Women
on the other hand were much more divided. Fifty-eight percent would shower regardless of time, but 40 percent said
they also enjoy a relaxing bubble bath.

Source: Zogby/America

up, you get in, and then you have to soak for 20 minutes. Who
has that kind of time?"

This preference for showering has led to the recent jump
in demand for shower columns and steam showers. A shower
column incorporates a fixed shower head along with a hand-
held shower wand and directionally adjustable body jets along
the column's length for full-body coverage. A steam shower
looks like a regular water shower, except it functions as a
ministeam room. However, the glass enclosure must extend to
the ceiling and the shower door has to be sealed. Proper installation and ventilation is crucial, however, so the steam doesn't
escape the shower and condense on the bathroom walls,
causing rot or mold.

Showering is so much in vogue right now that many
empty nesters with master suites are actually getting rid of
their bathtubs and replacing them with two-seater showers,
according to builder Steve Hendy. Another advantage of a
larger shower with a bench is that older homeowners find

them easier and safer to get into and out of. This is a trend that's sure to accelerate because every 7 seconds a new Baby Boomer turns 50, according to the U.S. Bureau of Labor and Statistics. This phenomenon is not slated to slow down until 2010.

4. *Install new flooring:* The paramount consideration in bathroom flooring is the safety of the product and its performance in a potentially wet environment. For these reasons, avoid wood, which stains in contact with water, and highly polished stone, which is extremely slippery when wet. Ceramic tile is popular in bathrooms, particularly the 18-inch and 20-inch

---

**TIPS: TEN WAYS TO LIGHT UP YOUR BATH**

1. *Shower power:* Lighting in the shower should be bright enough to help avoid spills while making shaving easier.
2. *Tub tip:* Recessed fixtures provide good general tub lighting.
3. *Window dressing:* Windows provide natural light to supplement electric options.
4. *Night bright:* Install linear lights in the toe-space below vanities and cabinets.
5. *Get glowing:* Indirect (cove) lighting adds a soft, warm glow.
6. *Mirror, mirror:* Vertical wall sconces flanking mirrors provide even facial lighting.
7. *Vanity fare:* A halogen light above the vanity provides cross illumination when used in tandem with wall sconces.
8. *Table topper:* Table lamps add a human touch to bathrooms. Display them away from water sources on tabletops or vanities.
9. *Ceiling star:* A decorative light fixture suspended from the ceiling provides an elegant touch while adding extra light.
10. *Potty panache:* Focused flood or halogen fixtures over the commode provide good light for reading.

Source: American Lighting Association

---

tiles set on a diagonal to make the room appear larger. When selecting ceramic tile, consider glazed porcelain tiles that are baked at a higher temperature, which makes them denser. The color also goes all the way through the tile, rather than just covering the surface, so nicks are not as visible.

5. *Update the lighting:* Today's more glamorous bathrooms demand more complex lighting solutions. Task lighting must be bright enough to do its job, but work well with indirect accent lighting designed to soften the room's ambiance by providing a warm glow.

Lighting fixtures and finishes should complement (rather than compete with) plumbing accessories, tile, paint, and wallpaper. New technology has added options as well. Fiber optics, with its remote light source, can create twinkling star effects when inset into bathroom ceilings.

# BASEMENT REMODEL

Contractors don't like to call them basements. "They're only basements until you remodel them," says Steve Hendy of Neal's Construction. "Then they become *lower levels.*"

Let's face it, basements suffer from an image problem. It's because we've all spent time in someone's dank, dark cavern watching a movie, shooting pool, playing cards, or maybe even playing air guitar after one too many beers. These poorly "remodeled" basements often smell of mildew, and the sight of painted concrete does nothing to blunt the impression you're spending time in what is basically a garage without the car.

Times have changed. Because new construction is so expensive, homeowners have rediscovered their basements where the walls, floors, ceilings, and access to the electrical and plumbing systems are already in place—and they're willing to shell out some serious cash to do the job right. That means installing a full bath! Basements are also the rooms that homeowners most often tackle themselves because they can spread out the work over a longer period of time without disrupting the rest of the household.

According to *Remodeling* magazine, the average basement remodel costs $43,865. The resale value of that remodel one year later is $34,801, an average return of 79 percent. While the specs for the magazine's project call for a wet bar, your lower level might include an exercise room, home office, kids' playroom, sauna, teen hangout, guest room, wine cellar, or home theater.

**Basement Remodel**

| Market | Job Cost | Resale Value | Cost Recouped |
|---|---|---|---|
| National average | $43,865 | $34,801 | 79 percent |

Source: *Remodeling* magazine, "2003 Cost vs. Value Report." Project description: Finish the lower level of a house to create a 20-by-30-foot entertaining area with wet bar, a 5-by-8-foot full bath, and a 12-by-12-foot auxiliary room. Walls and ceilings are painted drywall throughout; exterior walls are insulated, painted trim throughout. Include five six-panel primed hardboard doors. Main room shall include 15 recessed ceiling light fixtures and three-surface mounted light fixtures and snap-together laminate flooring system. Bathroom includes standard white toilet, vanity with cultured marble top, resilient vinyl flooring, two-piece fiberglass shower unit, a light/fan combination, vanity light fixture, and recessed medicine cabinet. Bar area includes 10 linear feet of raised-panel oak cabinets with laminate countertops, stainless steel bar sink, single-level bar faucet, undercounter refrigerator, and vinyl floor tile.

# FIVE BASEMENT REMODELING PROBLEMS YOU MUST OVERCOME

Every room presents its own special remodeling challenges, and the basement has more than its share. This is why it's so important not to cheat your budget here. If you don't refinish this room with the same like-quality materials as the rest of your home, then it will always remain a "basement" and never become the "lower level" of your dreams. When remodeling your basement, you might need to address one or more of the following problems:

- *Darkness:* Basements generally have fewer and smaller windows than the rest of your home, so don't skimp on the lighting. Incandescent recessed lights give off a brilliant white light and brighten the room. Additionally, maximize any available natural light either by enlarging basement windows where possible, or by tunneling sunlight from the roof to the basement stairway via a "skylight tube," a small (10- to 22-inch diameter) tube with a superreflective interior.

  The skylight tube features a clear, weatherproof dome on top that extends through the roof and a light diffuser on the bottom that mounts in the room's ceiling and looks like a standard ceiling light fixture. These tubes are particularly good for providing energy-efficient, natural lighting for entranceways, pantries, and stairwells. Some models include an exhaust vent fan for use in bathrooms and built-in electric lights for use at night.

- *Dampness:* Your lower level will never be more than a "cellar" until you take care of any moisture problems, whether they are caused by internal forces (condensation from humid air), external forces (poor grading or tiny leaks in the foundation), or a combination of the two. Wrapping pipes in insulation and running a dehumidifier should solve your condensation problems, as does occasionally cracking open a few basement windows when the dehumidifier is turned off.

  Fixing external water damage is usually more complicated and costly. It might be necessary to regrade the soil around your foundation so that it gradually slopes away from the house at a distance of two inches for every horizontal foot for a distance of three feet. Additionally, make sure your rain gutters are free of decaying leaves and other debris and that they empty away from your home's foundation. Standing water is an invitation to mold, a blight that can wreak havoc not only with the equity in your home, but your family's health as well.

Wet or damp carpet is a mold magnet, so forgo installing wall-to-wall in your basement and install vinyl or ceramic tile instead. If you must have some carpet, use area rugs instead. They will provide warmth and a decorative element, but they can be routinely pulled up and checked for mold or discarded if they get wet and cannot be cleaned.

- *Low ceilings:* To counteract the claustrophobic feeling of low basement ceilings, use horizontal lines that emphasize the room's length rather than vertical lines that highlight height. For example, setting floor tiles in a diagonal pattern will make the room feel wider. Don't install a suspended ceiling. They not only visually shorten a room that is already lacking height, they are completely passé. Lastly, hang any artwork slightly lower than you would on other floors of your home.

- *Ugly support columns, beams, and duct work:* Messing with your home's support system is generally never a good idea. Instead, conceal the worst visual offenders in soffits, walls, or built-in cabinets.

- *Ugly concrete walls:* There are two fixes for this problem and both camps have their fans and detractors: Those who advocate drywall and those who champion prefinished panels. While drywalling a basement is more time-consuming, paneling naysayers say drywall is more attractive and lasts longer. But paneling advocates say that the latest advances in building technology provide almost limitless options for dressing up your basement walls, including real wood mounted on plywood panels, simulated wood grain printed on paper and then fused to plywood panels, solid tongue-and-groove wood panels, and wallpaper panels that have a special clear topcoat.

Also gaining in popularity is the Owens Corning® Basement Finishing System. It consists of 4-by-8-foot fiberglass panels, snapped into PVC structural framing, that are damage, fire, and mold resistant. These "breathable" panels can be removed in order to access the interior foundation walls. Because the prefinished panels have built-in insulation and sound control properties, the system does not require additional insulation, drywall, taping, or painting.

# A WORD ABOUT FLOOR COVERINGS

Floor covering trends come and go much more slowly than other home improvements. According to D. Christopher Davis, the chief executive officer of the World Floor Covering Association, the average homeowner only changes the flooring in a room about once every 11 years when it "uglies out." While good looks is always a consideration in choosing a floor covering, it's actually more important that you select a floor that is compatible with your lifestyle. If you don't, the floor is likely to "ugly out" on you much more quickly. Ask any homeowner with one or more cats to describe the folly of installing ropelike sisal carpets! You might as well cover your floor with a giant scratching post. The carpet is sure to be ruined in no time at all.

If you are overwhelmed by the many choices of flooring available, there are several ways to narrow the field:

- Jot down what you like and don't like about the room's present floor covering.
- Clip pictures of flooring that you like from home and decorating magazines.
- Make a list of the pros, cons, and costs of each type of flooring for the room. (The chart on the next page can help.)

**The Pros, Cons, and Costs of Floor Covering**

Source: The World Floor Covering Association

| Type | Pros | Cons | Cost Per Square Foot |
|------|------|------|------|
| Carpet | Soft underfoot, many styles/colors/textures, noise absorbing, can be easily replaced. | Regular cleaning, might require restretching. | $1 to $5 |
| Ceramic | Many styles/colors, porcelain tile is particularly tough, glazed tile requires minimal maintenance. | No resilience, noisy, unglazed tiles require periodic sealing, hard and "cold" to the touch, grout should be sealed periodically, joints can leak to the subfloor. | $1 to $6 |
| Concrete | Can be textured, colored, mimic tile, works well with radiant heat system and passive solar designs, easily cleaned. | Needs frequent sealer to avoid wear pattern. | Varies |
| Cork | Soft and "spongy" underfoot, natural/durable material, "warm" to the touch, resists mildew, and does not absorb water. | Usually treated like wood, waxed cork needs occasional rewaxing and buffing. Not for heavy traffic areas. | $5 and up |
| Laminate | Can imitate many other flooring types (wood, tile, stone); easily installed, extremely durable. | Sound might appear "unreal." | $2 to $7 |
| Linoleum | Natural ingredients such as linseed oil, cork, tree resins; color goes all the way through. | Relatively expensive, professional installation only, need sealer, do not leave wet. | About $4 |

| | | | |
|---|---|---|---|
| **Natural Stone** | Natural material, "earthy" look, wide variety of textures | Some stone types require sealers, others require impregnation; avoid polished stone for safety. | $3 to $10 and up |
| **Vinyl** | Good looks, easy care, variety of textures and colors, water resistant in sheet form, soft underfoot, can imitate more expensive floor coverings. | Less expensive grades might discolor with age, susceptible to nicks and dents, can look artificial, nonabrasive cleaners only. | $1 to $5 |
| **Wood** | Various species, patterns, and styles; "rich" appearance; simple installation; mixes with any period style. | Requires regular maintenance, noisy, never wet mop, wipe up spills promptly, softwoods less durable than hardwoods. | $4 to $10 |

# CHAPTER 6

# HOME IMPROVEMENTS YOU SHOULDN'T BANK ON

## ALL HOME IMPROVEMENTS
## ARE *NOT* CREATED EQUAL

Let's face it. It's easy to get swept up in the home improvement craze. Your neighbors are remodeling their kitchen. Your sister-in-law is adding a bath. And your coworker is finishing his basement. You drive to work and every other house either has a dumpster in the front yard with an excavator next to it, or a pile of lumber sitting in the driveway.

Housing values are going up, but your stock portfolio has gone down. So now you're thinking about investing more money in your home. After all, a home is a sound investment and any home improvement is a good one. Right?

Wrong. While prices do head north on a steady basis (we've all read about homes in desirable vacation locations that have doubled in value in just a few years), not all home improvements are created equal.

## FIVE HOME IMPROVEMENTS THAT DON'T
## ALWAYS ADD VALUE TO YOUR HOME

We've learned that you can't contemplate each home improvement in a vacuum. For example, a family room is generally a good investment, but you have to consider what other features of your home are affecting its overall value. If your house has only one bathroom—and all the other houses in your neighborhood have two-and-a-half—do you really think you'll recoup over 75 percent of your investment in a new family room? (Highly doubtful.) You'd be much better off spending the money on adding a new bathroom. Chances are excellent you'll get a 95 percent return on that investment. (If not more!)

There are several home improvements that can go either way. You can't necessarily count on them to recoup a good return on your investment. But then again, you can't rule them out. They are:

1. *Adding several feet to one side of your home.* On the surface, this seems to make sense. Let's say your living room is just 11 feet wide and expanding it to 14 feet will square off the room and provide you with much more usable floor space. At the same time, you might also decide that you'll bump out the dining room so that you can get around the table without having to turn sideways.

   The problem with this type of addition is that its cost per square foot is likely to be extremely high. Remodeling typically costs 50 percent more than new construction. Every time contractors have to tie new construction into your existing home, the project gets trickier, takes more time to complete, and your costs tend to rise rather dramatically. This is because once the walls are opened up, you might encounter some unpleasant surprises. Sometimes the foundation is not square and, oftentimes, the walls are not plumb.

   You can save yourself a headache by simply adding another room or two rather than a little extra space to all the rooms. You might find that the cost per square foot is lower this way and that you'll get more usable space. Another bonus is that while the addition is underway, your family isn't as likely to be as disturbed by the construction because the contractors won't have to open up your home to the elements until the new room addition is well underway.

2. *Adding a pool.* Unless you live in an area of the country where pools are commonplace, don't add a pool to your home expecting a high rate of return. That's because adding pools—especially in-ground pools—often reduces the number of people who will consider buying your home. People who

don't like pools think of two things when they see one: maintenance and liability.

There is no doubt that having a pool requires a substantial investment of your time to maintain it. There is the vacuuming, checking the filter, adding chemicals, opening the pool, closing the pool—the list goes on and on. In-ground pools can be even worse. A potential homebuyer can envision taking down an above-ground pool and regrading the yard, but instinctively recognizes that removing an in-ground pool is much more challenging and costly. And he or she doesn't even want to think about the potential for a lawsuit. (See Chapter 12.)

3. *Adding high-end accessories to an average home.* Most people view home as their refuge, their place to relax and get away from it all. It is indeed important to make your home comfortable for you and your family. But at the same time, you need a good idea of how your home might be viewed one day by potential buyers.

If you want to add some of the following high-end accessories to your home because you really want them, that's fine. Just don't expect much of a return from your investment should you decide to sell. Be wary of adding:

- **High-end built-in appliances.** The popularity of cooking shows on television certainly hasn't hurt those remodelers who focus on kitchens. But you have to match the quality of appliances to the quality of the room, the house, and neighborhood. This doesn't mean you pick out bargain-basement appliances when remodeling your kitchen, but perhaps the Miele dishwasher is more than you need for your kitchen that's mainly furnished with Kenmore appliances. It also means that if you're getting ready-made cabinets off the floor of your local home improvement store, adding a commercial grade stove that costs $6000 and a refrigerator that costs $4000 doesn't make much economic sense. Although these features might be desirable to potential homebuyers, you will only get a fraction of your original purchase price at resale because these high-end appliances just don't fit the house or the neighborhood.

- **Exotic, hand-painted tile.** Although you might love the design, potential homebuyers might not. And they might be thoroughly intimidated by the thought of tackling a tile removal project so soon after buying a new house.

- **Central vacuum.** This is another high-end accessory that might not give you much bang for your remodeling buck. It can be costly to add the piping throughout your home. In addition, with most folks' hectic lifestyles, many people would rather spend that money on a cleaning service and let the professionals worry about schlepping the vacuum up and down the stairs.

4. *Adding central air conditioning.* If adding central air conditioning comes at the expense of premium closet space, you might do more harm than good to the value of your home. Many older homes are built with limited closet space. Taking up valuable space to add central air can cause new storage problems. If you're thinking of adding central air, make sure you talk with contractors who understand how to cool your home without taking away your valuable closet space.

5. *Adding new windows.* Unless your present windows are literally falling out or won't operate, replacement windows won't recoup the significant investment you'll need to make to buy those new tilt-in, high-efficiency windows. An average-sized, high-efficiency double-hung window can easily cost you $200 (high-end models can cost 50 percent more) and installation per window can be about the same. Add up all the windows in your house and you will see the kind of hit you'll take in the pocketbook. If you have 10 windows on one floor—that's $2000 in windows alone.

Cheap replacement windows can save you money in the short run. However, cheap replacement windows often have wide sashes that cut down on the amount of glass, thus darkening your home. Real estate pros will tell you that bright, cheery homes outsell dark, somber ones every time.

# A WORD ABOUT SIDING

Siding is one of those improvements (like putting in a new pool) that might or might not return a sizable portion of your original investment. According to *Remodeling* magazine, installation of new vinyl siding with trim on a 1250 square-foot home returned an average of 98 percent in 2003. But how much *you* will recoup depends on where you live, the condition of your home, what kind of siding you install, and whether property values are rising or falling in your neighborhood. Siding, however, has two main advantages over interior improvements: It actually decreases home maintenance and it has huge curb appeal.

"Siding is *all* about curb appeal," says Stephen Gladstone, president of the American Society of Home Inspectors. According to Gladstone, after potential buyers consider a home's location, its school district, and count the bedrooms and bathrooms, "ultimately it comes down to whether the home looks neat and clean,"—both inside and out. Siding goes a long way toward delivering this pretty picture. Siding's other big plus is that it helps "blend in" an addition with the rest of the home. It provides a seamless visual transition from the old portion of the existing home to the new.

| Siding Replacement | | | |
|---|---|---|---|
| Market | Job Cost | Resale Value | Cost Recouped |
| National average | $7,329 | $7,247 | 98 percent |

Source: *Remodeling* magazine, "2003 Cost vs. Value Report." Project description: Replace 1250 square feet of existing siding with new vinyl siding, including all trim.

Which kind of siding is the best investment for your home? Again, there are many factors involved, including your home's location, what type of siding your neighbors have, and your budget. Additionally, it's often hard to predict the tastes of potential buyers. Gladstone says that while one homebuyer looks at a vinyl-sided house and says, "No, it looks too plastic," another homebuyer looks at the same house and says, "Great! Now I don't have to paint." The chart on the next page highlights the pros and cons of the most popular siding options.

As with all home improvements, you must do your homework before choosing siding. Some materials, such as synthetic stucco, can turn your home improvement into a nightmare, says Gladstone. Synthetic stucco, also known as Exterior Insulation and Finishing System (EIFS), is a multilayer product that produces an attractive stonelike finish. It gained widespread popularity in the United States in the 1980s as an economical alternative to real stucco, which is generally made of cement, sand, hydrated lime, and water.

However, a significant number of homeowners (particularly in the southern states) started complaining of moisture and mold damage to their synthetic stucco-covered homes. It was discovered that when the fake stucco is applied to a home's exterior, the EIFS layers bond to form an airtight covering. If water breaches the system, those layers can trap moisture, which then soaks into the wood framing and causes the wood to rot. Mold and termites might ensue, spawning damage that might destroy a home if left unchecked.

Although damage caused by synthetic stucco has been the subject of hundreds of lawsuits, the manufacturers of the product deny that it is defective. The product's advocates have squarely placed the blame for any problems on the contractors who apply the system incorrectly. Although synthetic stucco is often the focus of homeowners' horror stories, keep in mind that *any* type of siding that is improperly applied or inadequately maintained can cause you countless headaches and drastically reduce the curb appeal and value of your home.

| Siding Type | Pros | Cons |
|---|---|---|
| Aluminum | Low maintenance. Can be painted if color change is desired. | Easily dented or damaged. Color changes due to weather exposure are common. Painted siding might "chalk" (deteriorate and turn dusty) with age. |
| Cedar or redwood boards | Higher-grade woods can last 50 years when properly maintained. Real wood appearance. | Higher cost for materials and requires sealing, staining, or painting to maintain. Subject to damage by bees, squirrels, and woodpeckers. |
| Cement board | Resistant to decay, weathering, and pest infestation. Wood-grain appearance. | Has to be painted and maintained every five to seven years. Installation costs might be higher than aluminum or vinyl. |
| Fiberboard panels | Lower cost for materials and installation. Might be painted to change colors. | Exposed edges are subject to weathering and decay. Contact with concrete, roofing, or improper installation can expose material to water and mold. Nails and screws must be sealed and maintained to keep out water. |
| Vinyl | Lower cost for materials and installation. Color changes due to weather are uncommon. Is available with wood grain appearance in a variety of colors. Can be painted to change colors. | Weather changes might cause vinyl to expand and contract, exposing overlapping joints. Subject to damage from rocks thrown up by lawnmowers or melting from outdoor grills placed too close to the house. |

# CHAPTER 7

# HEATING AND AIR CONDITIONING: STAYING WARM AND KEEPING COOL

# FROM AFTERTHOUGHT TO CENTER STAGE

With the rates of childhood asthma more than doubling since 1980, and folks suffering year round from various respiratory ailments due to allergies and second-hand smoke, indoor air quality in the home has taken on crucial importance. This means heating and air conditioning for homes and additions has gone from a mere afterthought to a key element in planning for new construction. But what does this mean for you and the return on your home improvements?

If you already have a hot-air system in your home, you should expand it into your addition because hot air systems can now be outfitted with various filter systems that control the degree of humidity and the amount of airborne dust particles inside your home. If you have a hot-water heating system and are building a large addition, you might want to consider adding a separate hot-air unit to the new construction. This will make it easier to heat the space in a more efficient and cost-effective manner. In turn, this will add to the resale value of your home. Most new hot-air furnaces exhaust through the wall using plastic pipe, making installation a snap.

Another choice is to add an in-wall heat pump unit like those commonly found in hotel rooms. These units can be more efficient to run, especially if your furnace is a great distance from the addition itself.

When it comes to cooling, central air conditioning units are quieter and much more energy efficient than portable units. Another air conditioning choice is an in-wall unit. If you install one of these (instead of putting one in the window), be sure to select one that has a removable chassis so that, if you need to repair the unit, it can be slid out of the sleeve that remains in the wall. In terms of resale value and appeal to potential homebuyers, central air adds the most value to your home, followed by in-wall units, and then window units.

A word of caution: Be sure to size the air conditioning unit properly. A unit that's too large for the space will cool it too quickly and won't remove much humidity from the air, causing condensation on windows and walls. A unit that is too small will tax the appliance and won't cool the room enough during a prolonged heat wave. And no matter what the season, make sure to have your HVAC (heating, ventilation, and air conditioning) equipment routinely inspected by a certified HVAC professional.

Mold can grow abundantly inside heating and cooling equipment if it has food to eat (airborne dust) and moisture. The moisture might come from high indoor humidity or water leaks into the HVAC system and ducts. Once you have a mold infestation problem in your HVAC system, you are in danger of contaminating your entire home as mold spores are continually circulated through the home and back into the HVAC system through return registers and ducts.

## REVIEW HEAT LOSS

Anytime you add on, you should conduct a heat-loss review of your home and the proposed addition to ensure that your current heating and air conditioning units can handle the additional square footage. Because additions commonly have three walls detached from the existing structure, their heating and cooling requirements are often different from the rest of your home. You might want to consider adding a separate heating and air conditioning zone so that your new room or rooms are comfortable. This is especially true for additions on the north side of the house in cooler climates and the south side of the house in warmer climates. It will cost you a little more money to add a new zone, but it will be money well spent.

Hot-air furnaces generally possess about 10 to 15 percent extra capacity. So if your addition only increases the size of your home by this percentage, your furnace might be quite capable of carrying the added load, according to builder Alan Hanbury. Hanbury says that hot water or steam furnaces generally have 30 to 40 percent additional capacity so that much larger additions can be supported without changing the size of the boiler. In any event, completing a thorough heat-loss review of your existing home and proposed addition is imperative. The last thing you want to do is start cutting into your new walls, floors, and ceilings to upgrade your HVAC system if your budget is already tight.

# REEXAMINE YOUR WATER HEATER

Your water heater is another part of your heating system that is often overlooked. All too often, homeowners get excited about their new whirlpools or bubble tubs only to discover in the midst of filling their new pride and joy that their 30-gallon water heater can't do the job. Lukewarm bubbles just don't do the trick for your aching muscles.

If you are putting in a big tub, make sure your water heater is properly sized. You might even want to look into tankless water heaters that can deliver piping hot water for your bath. If your tub holds more than 30 gallons (or you are considering a shower with multiple heads), you might want to consider talking to your contractor or plumber about increasing the size of the water supply lines to your new bathroom. This can sometimes get very expensive, as new lines might have to go all the way back to where water enters your house. But, again, think resale value: If the multiple-head shower only trickles water, how impressed do you think any prospective homebuyer will be? They will likely start looking for more things that might be wrong with your house.

**R You Savvy about Windows?** The energy performance of a window is measured by its R-value. The higher the R-value, the more the window will protect you against heat-loss and shield you from the sun's glare. A standard single-pane window has an R-value of about 0.9. An insulated glass window—two panes of glass separated by airspace—has an R-value of nearly 2.

**Note:** The frame also affects the window's R-value. Wood, fiberglass, and plastic frames insulate better against heat than standard metal frames. To improve the performance of metal frames, make sure they have a thermal break, a strip of insulating plastic inside the frame.

## CONSIDER ENERGY EFFICIENCY

Predicting the future is dicey business, but you have to agree that energy costs have a much better chance of increasing than decreasing, perhaps dramatically so. If you are going to build an addition, you will want to consider energy savings not only for resale value, but also to cut your energy expenses.

How do you do that? You will likely be building a much more energy efficient space than what is in your current home, particularly if your home is more than 10 years old. You will be using 2-x-6 construction with 6 inches of insulation in the walls and 12 inches in the ceiling. But there are some other ways you can cut your energy consumption:

- Use house wrap to cover the sheathing before you add the siding. You'll appreciate the added comfort on windy days.
- Use double-pane low emissivity (low-E) windows. Low-E windows have an invisible coating on the inside of the glass

that reflects heat, keeping your house warmer in winter and cooler in summer.

- Check the R-value of windows you plan to install. Higher numbers mean better protection.

- Ask your contractor to use a foam seal where the sill plate meets the concrete foundation or frost wall.

- Put foam seals around your plugs and switches on exterior walls before putting the switch plates on them.

- Consider building an overhang for south-facing windows so that the summer sun won't cause excessive glare, while still allowing the winter sun to peek in.

- Minimize north-facing windows in cooler climates.

- Check the R-value on exterior doors and garage doors. Some models on the market today insulate as well as a new wall.

- If you add a traditional fireplace, keep the flue shut when not in use. And if you add gas logs to the fireplace, look for logs that don't require you to leave the flue open when not in use. (Leaving the flue open pulls heated air out of your house 24 hours a day. It's equal to leaving a window open.)

- If you add a gas fireplace, choose one that takes combustion air from outside with little leakage to your indoor environment. Adding a blower to the unit will dramatically increase heat output.

- Insulate floors over unheated areas.

# CHAPTER 8

# LANDSCAPE AND HARDSCAPE: IT DON'T MEAN A THING IF YOU AIN'T GOT THAT SWING

# HELLO HARDSCAPE

Once upon a time, landscaping was simple. We threw down some grass seed, poured a concrete sidewalk, planted a few bushes, and added some petunias in the summer for a splash of color. Today, it's easy for our senses (and credit cards) to be overwhelmed by the multitude of choices we have to extend our living space outdoors. Just take a look at what your local lawn and garden center is stocking these days. Yes, there are plants, but also bricks, pavers, pottery, arbors, fences, edging, outdoor fireplaces, and koi pools. And don't forget the decorative fountains, birdbaths, swings, gliders, gazebos, and patio furniture.

"It used to be four shrubs on the left and four shrubs on the right," says Don Woods, president of Stonehedge Landscaping and Garden Center in Newington, Connecticut. "Most people don't want that anymore." According to Woods, as the average size of homes has grown in the past 30 years, so has the budget and complexity of most landscaping jobs.

Whereas three decades ago, a homeowner might spend a couple hundred dollars on landscaping, today many professionally designed landscaping projects begin around $3500 and can quickly balloon to $10,000 or more.

---

**Go-go Garden Gnomes.** According to the National Gardening Association and Harris Interactive, 85 million U.S. households spent $39.6 billion at lawn and garden retail outlets in 2002, while 24.7 million households spent $28.9 billion on professional landscaping, lawn, and tree-care services.

---

Just what is driving the boon in landscape spending these days? Woods says it is homeowners who are anxious to update their "hardscapes," the inanimate elements of their landscapes, such as brick pathways, decks, porches, and patios. Homeowners are tearing out their old concrete and asphalt sidewalks and driveways with a vengeance. They're replacing them with colorful pavers, complete with "soldier courses" flanking the outer edges, giving them an old-fashioned appearance much like cobblestone.

# PAVER PARTICULARS

The explosion in the popularity of pavers can be witnessed at any home improvement and garden center. Piled on pallets right to the rooftops, pavers come in a variety of shapes and sizes and a rainbow of colors. Stone pavers that are tumbled to give them a distressed look are especially in demand.

Pavers are enjoying widespread appeal because today's products are extremely durable, says Woods. The density of pavers exceeds traditional blacktop so they can be used in driveways that are plowed in the colder climates—as long as the base upon which they sit has been adequately prepared. "The base is the entire success of your walk," says Woods. The homeowners who run into trouble with their paving project are those who don't prepare the base deep enough and subsequently encounter problems with water or frost heaves.

---

**TIP:** *Make sure any stone or brick products that you put in the ground are designed for this purpose. Most bricks are not made to be put in the ground and might crack or crumble over time, creating unsightly and unsafe walkways.*

*Likewise, make sure any wood you use for edging is pressure treated, otherwise it will only be a temporary edging solution.*

---

Pavers cost from $2 to $7 per square foot, and labor to install them can range from $6 to $18 per square foot. You can save on labor if you are willing to do the job yourself and do it the right way, which means adequate project preparation. Woods recommends:

- Excavating the base to 1 foot deep.
- Adding eight inches for ¾-inch process stone.
- Adding 2 inches of sand.
- Laying the pavers, usually measuring 2 inches high.

While some might say that excavating the base to 12 inches deep is excessive, Woods remains unfazed. "We don't get a lot of callbacks," he says simply. And no matter how beautiful your new front walkway looks when the last paver is set in place, it won't add any value to your home a year later if the pavers are all pushed up or there are huge gaps between them.

# LANDSCAPE APPEAL

Nothing adds to the curb appeal of your home quite like attractive landscaping. The variety of plants available to homeowners today is staggering. According to Woods, 30 years ago, practically everyone had junipers and yews in their yards. "We don't even stock these anymore," he says.

With the proliferation of mail-order catalogues and Internet shopping, homeowners now have at their fingertips everything from traditional evergreen bushes to fancy ornamental grasses that provide visual appeal to their home's terrain. Plants, bushes, and flowers are sold everywhere—from the nursery, to home improvement centers, to the grocery store. The key to making a wise investment is to spend time researching the plants that are appropriate for your climate and sun and soil conditions. When you are ready to buy, make sure you

Did you ever put in black plastic edging along your flowerbeds or lawn in order to get that finished look—only to have it pop out of the ground later on? It's a common (and aggravating) problem, but there is a solution. Instead of buying plastic edging in rolls from the home improvement store, spend the extra money to get the heavier-grade plastic edging sold in straight 20-foot sections from the nurseries. Because it is shipped flat, it doesn't have the "memory" that causes it to pull up out of the ground.

select plants that look healthy. Avoid buying any plant with yellow or drooping foliage. While good-quality plants cost a few dollars more, the plants will repay you by looking great for years to come.

# MULCH MATTERS

One of the quickest ways to improve your home's outward appearance (and therefore its value) is to spread new mulch around your bushes. Try it! It makes the rest of your landscaping look brand new.

Stone has fallen out of favor with many homeowners as a natural substance to control the weeds around the plantings. This is because the stones find their way onto the grass where they are soon kicked up by lawn mowers. Instead, mulch has become a much more popular choice, particularly double-ground pine bark. Although some of Woods' customers prefer cedar mulch because they believe it will last longer, the landscaper disagrees. He says that pine mulch lies flatter, is more attractive, and has the same insect-repelling qualities.

According to Woods, red mulch is also falling out of favor with homeowners because they are tiring of the "dyed" look. They are also concerned about finding bits of metal strapping and and nails mixed in due to the fact that red mulch is made up of a variety of recycled products, including ground-up pallets, pressure treated timber, and even construction debris.

# AN OUTDOOR ROOM OF ONE'S OWN

Seventy years ago, nearly every home had a front porch. After supper, parents sat out on the porch socializing with their neighbors while the kids played ball or tag on the lawn. These porches were simple, consisting of a couple of chairs and a light for those nights when the conversation carried on past dark.

Today's porches (patios, decks, and three-season rooms) are nothing like that. Now homeowners are taking these leisure spaces and transforming them into "outdoor rooms"—backyard escapes that often include high-end barbecues that cost as much as commercial-grade ovens, outdoor furniture that looks and feels more like family room furniture, sound systems, dinner tables, refrigerators, and hot tubs. These outdoor rooms can help create a backyard oasis. Here adults can unwind after a hard day at work and children can play with their friends.

---

**Wicker anyone?** As the popularity of outdoor rooms continues to grow, so do the sales of outdoor furniture. By 2006, retail sales of outdoor and casual furniture will climb to $4 billion, up from $3 billion in 2002, according to the U.S. Outdoor and Casual Furniture Report.

And speaking of outdoor and casual furniture, if you love the look of wicker, but don't appreciate the squeak and the upkeep, then consider buying synthetic wicker. It is more durable and practically maintenance free. Cushions for synthetic wicker often include outdoor options that are moisture resistant and come in a variety of designer colors and patterns.

---

If you want to increase the value of your home and its interior is already in good shape, you might want to consider investing some of your money in upgrading your "outdoor living spaces"—or adding a new outdoor room of your own. A charming patio or well-appointed three-season room could mean the difference between a quick home sale for your asking price, or your home languishing on the market while other homes with such amenities sell briskly.

First you need to decide how much you will use your new "room." Should it be a screened-in porch for warm weather use only? Or should it be a three-season room with windows that allow you to keep your furniture in place year round? Or perhaps you want a four-season room, complete with a heating source for year-round use with removable windows so that only the screens are in place during the summer months. Whichever option you choose, you must do your homework as carefully as if you were planning an interior room. Make sure you:

- Consider orientation. The north side of your house is the best place to put your room if you want to stay cool. If the room faces south, awnings or shades will be necessary to keep the afternoon heat and glare from overwhelming you.

- Add adequate lighting so that the room can be used after dark. If the room is fully enclosed, add enough electrical outlets for such essentials as floor lamps and small appliances like a coffeemaker or minifridge. And don't forget that adding a porch will reduce the amount of light coming into the room to which it's attached, so you must plan to install additional lighting in that room, too.

- Consider adding some type of sound system. You might use a boombox or outdoor speakers that are connected to your interior sound system.

- Consider your cooling needs. *Trading Spaces* aside, ceiling fans are the most popular choices.

- Consider the room's layout. Remember back in Chapter 4 we said the flow of an addition is crucial to getting the maximum value of your home at resale? Well the same is true for the flow of your outdoor room. Putting in a glass sliding door that gives you easy access to the backyard will help give your room the open and airy look that today's homebuyers are looking for.

- Consider the cost. A simple 10-by-12-foot porch can cost as little as $5000, while a 16-by-24-foot four-season room can set you back $30,000 or more.

# A WORD ABOUT DECKS

The development of pressure-treated lumber created an explosion in the number of decks attached to homes in the 1980s and 1990s. Before then, people just put lawn chairs out in the backyard or built small decks out of pine. In a few years, however, that pine deck began to age rather poorly, was the source of numerous splinters, and generally became a detriment to the value of a home rather than an asset.

Pressure treated lumber, first with a 20-year guarantee and then later with a 40-year guarantee, was just what homeowners were looking for. It was solid, attractive, and promised to last virtually forever. And while pressure-treated lumber will outlast its untreated counterpart, it is certainly not maintenance-free. You need to seal, stain, or paint your deck at least every other year.

Decks have undergone a transformation from simple, slightly elevated platforms to multilevel masterpieces. They are no longer just a place for that webbed lawn furniture. Today they're designed for quality furniture, potted plants, as well as separate sitting, eating, and grilling areas. And while the average deck used to be about 10-by-12 square feet, today they are often twice and three times as large.

But what will make your deck add value to your home? First of all, it must be well constructed and fit in with the look of your home and yard. It must have the proper flow from your home. Before construction, consider:

- What design works best for your home? Multiple levels can provide a classic look, but be sure each level is large enough to accomplish its designated task.

- How will you access your deck from inside your home? Sliding glass doors or swinging French doors help provide an open and airy look.

- How will you access your deck from the outside? You need to make it easy for you and your guests to gain access to your deck from the lawn.

- How high will your deck be elevated off of the ground? The higher the deck, the more dangerous it can be and the more important will be the security of the railing. Once your deck is elevated more than a foot, consider adding lattice to block the view under your deck.

- What style railing do you want? The easiest way to change the look of any deck is to change the railings. There are a wide variety of balusters available, in a variety of materials, that can provide you with either a traditional or contemporary look.

So a good deck will increase the value of your home, possibly recouping your full investment. A poor one will cost you money at resale. No homeowner wants the headache and expense of dealing with a rotted, splintering, moldy block of wood that looks like it was just slapped onto the side of your house. This is one home improvement where you sure don't want to prove you belong to the category of the "substantially unhandy" of whom home inspector Steve

**Deck Addition**

| Market | Job Cost | Resale Value | Cost Recouped |
|---|---|---|---|
| National average | $6,304 | $6,661 | 104 percent |

Source: *Remodeling* magazine, "2003 Cost vs. Value Report." Project description: Add a 16-by-20-foot deck using pressure treated pine joists supported by 4- × -4 posts set into concrete footings. Install composite deck material in a simple linear pattern. Include a built-in bench and planter of the same decking material. Provide a complete railing system using either a matching system made of the same composite as the decking material or a compatible vinyl system.

Gladstone spoke in Chapter 5. If you're not a home improvement professional, hire one to build your deck.

While decks are still extremely popular improvements, more homeowners are adding roofs over them and screening them in. These screen rooms offer protection from the elements and insects, giving homeowners additional opportunities to use them. And as more articles about the threat of the West Nile Virus appear, this trend is only likely to increase. (According to the U.S. Centers for Disease Control, West Nile Virus, a seasonal infection transmitted by mosquitoes, grew from an initial U.S. outbreak of 62 disease cases in 1999 to 4156 reported cases, including 284 deaths, in 2002.) So while building a simple deck might suit your needs today, consider fronting the extra money to screen it in now or plan on doing so in the immediate future.

# PART 3

# STAY THE COURSE

# CHAPTER 9

# READY, SET, SPEND!

# THINKING IT ALL THROUGH

So you have a home improvement idea, some money, a hammer, some nails, and you're ready to start your project. Great! Now put all that stuff away and let's think this thing through.

If you simply can't stand the orange countertops in your kitchen or your family room with the black paint and mural of the moon on the walls, then go ahead and get busy. Pretty much anything you do here will update your home's look. Aesthetic improvements, such as removing hideous wallpaper, buying a new refrigerator, or painting the walls, are relatively easy to complete, and they don't have to be permanent. On the other hand, elaborate improvements, such as building a large addition, can take six months or more to finish. If you don't plan them carefully, you might wind up ripping out your improvement or hiring someone to correct the design flaws. Either way, you can end up wasting your hard-earned dollars.

To properly prepare for a home improvement project, you should spend at least twice the amount of time it will take you to finish the project on the planning stage itself. If it's going to take you *three* days to install crown molding in your living room and paint the walls, you should spend a minimum of *six* days gathering paint samples, looking at molding styles, and researching design features that will work well in your home. The reason why you need so much time to plan is that it helps you uncover the glitches—large and small—that are inherent in the home improvement process.

Take Dan's first addition, for example. Several years ago, Dan and his wife Janet decided they would replace their screened-in porch with a 14-by-12-foot sunroom. First they looked at prefabricated models. Then they went to the library and checked out books on remodeling. They bought magazines. They talked to friends. They went to home shows—and returned with a lot of key chains and paint stirrers, as well as ideas. After six months of exploring prefabricated sunrooms, they decided this type of improvement really wouldn't fit their needs. The room was bound to be too hot in the summer and too cold in the winter.

After further discussion, they decided to stick-build a room with windows on all sides. Then their builder reminded them that they were already pulling their shades down in their living room each afternoon to stop the glare, so windows on all three sides of the addition wouldn't make sense. As a compromise, Dan and Janet went with a big bay window in the front of their addition and a large picture window in the back. When their builder also pointed out how quickly the grade in their backyard dropped off, they also quickly abandoned their original idea to put the addition on a slab in order to save money. (The frost wall would have been four feet deep at the house and more than six feet deep at its furthest point.) While thinking it all through, they realized it made more sense to put in a 22-by-16-foot addition with a full foundation and a basement and take advantage of the added space for storage.

If Dan and Janet had jumped out of bed one morning, grabbed the Yellow Pages and immediately let their fingers do the walking, they would have been unhappy with their new room in short order. They would have built a small sunroom (with no additional storage space) that baked in the afternoon sun and was too cold to use in the winter. Instead, they built a good-sized room that continues to meet their family's needs. And who knows? Dan and Janet might even decide to turn it into their first-floor master suite as they grow older and their kids leave home.

## FIVE STEPS TO GET GOOD REMODELING RESULTS

To keep your sanity during the crucial planning stages of the project (and protect your pocketbook when the hammers start to fly) follow this five-step process:

1. *Determine what features in your current home aren't working for you.* Find some quiet time to sit down and think about what works in your house and what doesn't. Ask your spouse or partner to do the same. Compare notes. Discuss your dreams of your ideal home. Remember, there aren't any bad ideas during this brainstorming part of your planning. You aren't going to run out tomorrow and start knocking down walls; you just need to have an open and honest discussion. For example, ask yourselves:

   - Do I like to host gatherings for my family and friends? Do I have the room to invite as many people over as I would like?
   - Have I been drooling over a 50-inch plasma screen television and will the room I am thinking of building support such a large TV?
   - Is the flow of my home conducive to conversation when people come over to visit?
   - Do my family and friends frequently stay overnight? Do I have room for them to stay without disrupting the entire house?
   - Can I walk through my living room or family room without stepping on toys—or piled-up books and CDs?
   - Are my clothes stored in my bedroom closet or scattered in various closets and boxes throughout the house?
   - Do I (or any other members of my family) like to shop for a lot of clothes?
   - Are there too many people for the number of bathrooms in my house?
   - Is my galley kitchen cramping my gourmet cooking talent?
   - Is Thanksgiving dinner at my house served in three separate sittings?
   - Do my children have to sleep in bunk beds when they would prefer not to?

   Take a long, hard look at how your house meets your needs—and how it doesn't. And don't forget to plan 5, 10, or even 20 years in advance whenever possible.

2. *Realistically discuss what is missing from your home.* You might want a 5000-square-foot home, but is that what you really need and are willing to fund? If you have one child and don't have many overnight guests, do you really need four or five bedrooms? If you're disappointed that you can't host your entire family for the holidays, perhaps you can throw an outdoor Fourth of July celebration and let Aunt Stella feed the clan in her huge recreation room.

   Your top priority is to address your everyday needs and not just your occasional wishes or desires. We said earlier that people are no longer installing huge whirlpool tubs in their bathrooms coupled with tiny stall showers. This is because most people use their whirlpools infrequently, but shower daily. Make sure your house meets your daily needs first. It can only help to increase your home's resale value.

3. *Hit the road.* No, that doesn't mean you should get out of town before you do something crazy. To get good ideas, you can:
   - Talk with family and friends about their homes.
   - Visit open houses. It's often tough to visualize changes to your home. At an open house, you can see new ideas in person.
   - Attend a home show. Stop to browse through the display books. Contractors will be there to show off their best ideas. Learn from them.
   - Buy magazines, visit the library, browse in bookstores, search the Internet, and watch some home improvement shows. Learn the current trends as well as what has stood the test of time. This is what will help you to increase the value of your home.

4. *Keep an open mind.* You might have your heart set on a particular design feature, but if the plan is flawed, you will need to modify it. Have faith; your finished project will be much better than your original idea.

5. *Set a realistic time horizon.* It's human nature to want the things we're craving right away, but your home improvement has to fit into your family and your professional life. If your daughter is getting married in May and you will be hosting several parties, do you want contractors to start remodeling your kitchen in April?

Depending on the type and extent of your home improvement, it is important to realize that this process can be extremely stressful. Make sure you're ready for the disruption to all your lives.

# WHO WILL ACTUALLY DO THE WORK?

Now it's time to figure out exactly who will transform your dreams into reality. You have three basic choices:

- **Roll up your sleeves and get to work.** Remember when you could stop by a Lowe's or Home Depot after 8 p.m., get what you needed, and get out? Not anymore. Now that home improvement has become our national pastime, these stores are almost never quiet. Today, millions of handy people are painting bedrooms, tiling floors, and installing new kitchen cabinets. But wait a minute. Just because you're a pro at installing closet organizers, do you really think you're ready to tackle a 500-square-foot addition? Better think twice.

  You need to know your strengths *and* weaknesses as a handy person. You might already live in a house (or know somebody who lives in a house) where the previous owner did all the remodeling without any help—and it shows. Horribly. From the half-painted windows, to the sander marks on the oak floors, to the faucet that always drips, this is one homeowner who should have hired a professional.

  In addition, remember that large home improvement projects take time—time that you won't have for reading the

> **Reminder:** The resale values of remodeling jobs quoted in this book are for jobs done to professional standards, with no defects. The return on your remodeling investments will be reduced if your improvements are not professionally completed. Any construction or remodeling done poorly will hurt the value of your home.

newspaper, playing with the kids, getting ahead at work, watching television, going out to dinner with friends, taking vacations, lounging by the pool, or anything else that you like to do in your spare time. The more work you do on your own, the more money you will save (provided you don't commit a costly blunder), but it will cost you more in time. Only you can decide whether it is worth it.

If you are unsure whether you can do the job yourself, ask your family and friends what they think. Ask yourself whether you have the time to devote to this project or whether your time would be better spent furthering your career or spending more time with your family.

• **You serve as the general contractor.** This is a scaled-back version of the first option. Instead of doing all of the work yourself, you hire subcontractors to do the jobs requiring the greatest degree of skill.

If you like the idea of controlling exactly who is working on your house (and have a job that allows you the flexibility to meet with contractors at all hours of the day), then you might want to consider this option. On average, general contractors receive about 15 to 20 percent of the total cost of the project to manage the job. That fee pays for meetings with the homeowner, ordering materials, and coordinating the subcontractors. But the job can get stressful if problems start cropping up and the schedule gets further and further behind. Serving as the general contractor tends to work best for those who have prior building experience, know at least two of the subcontractors hired for the job, and for those who have a lot of patience.

It's a law of nature: When you are renovating, things *will* go wrong. Then the subcontractors will look to you to sort things out. For example, if you hire an architect who hasn't worked with the framer, they might not communicate well with each other. While the plans might seem straightforward to the architect, the framer might interpret them differently, order the wrong materials, and soon everyone is frustrated and annoyed.

On the other hand, this option allows you to select the subcontractors whom you want to work on your home based on the quality of their work and their prices. Of course the downside is that if you live in a region where all the subcontractors are in high demand, you might very well run into scheduling nightmares.

Scheduling is one of the biggest challenges when you serve as your own general contractor. Some of the subcontractors you hire might be getting a third or more of their work from a single general contractor. If that contractor needs something done quickly, which job do you think will get preference? Also, even if you have a set schedule and can get the subcontractors to comply, if just one of them fails to show up, it can put a crimp into the rest of the project.

- **Hire a design-build firm to do the job.** Twenty years ago, there were just a handful of design-build firms. Now they're popping up all across the country. Featuring one-stop shopping, design-build firms provide everything from the architect to the painter. Some even provide interior design services.

  What are the benefits of working with a design-build firm? If you have ever witnessed a bunch of subcontractors jabbing their fingers at each other as they assess blame for something that has gone wrong, you know the concept is a good one. Hiring a design-build firm does not ensure that you will get your home improvement finished in the time frame you decided upon without any problems. However, you will get a professional to manage the project's flow from start to finish.

Caution, though: There are big differences between one design-build firm and another. Some design-build firms can save you money. The better ones take the time to investigate what isn't working in your home and why. Then they design an efficient and aesthetically pleasing solution. Because remodeling is their livelihood, these professionals tend to be more objective about the process than the homeowners who hire them. They can also step back and envision the entire project from planning stage to completion.

For example, after first meeting with homeowners, builder Alan Hanbury meets with them again to show them four to six different options for the completed project. Each option reduces the price of the project by eight to 10 percent. "Then I can match [the customer's] ideas and priorities to stay in budget," says Hanbury.

If you and your spouse or partner work long hours, or if neither of you has the experience or the desire to manage a home improvement project, this is the option for you. Hiring a design-build firm means that you will have one point of contact, one person to go to with your concerns, and one person who coordinates the job from initial planning to the end.

Remember, though, that hiring a design-build firm doesn't guarantee you that the job will start and end on time and on budget, nor does it guarantee you that all of the work will be done to the highest standards. Just like in your profession, there are those who are truly committed to outstanding work. Then there are some folks who do average work. And, unfortunately, there are those who do poor work. Your job is to educate yourself so that you avoid the remodelers who fall into the third category.

**DIY or Not?** Should you save money by doing the job yourself? Do-it-yourself (DIY) jobs are a popular trend in the home improvement industry. However, before you grab a hammer and start swinging, the National Association of the Remodeling Industry (NARI) recommends that you take this DIY quiz. Answer "Yes" or "No."

- Do you enjoy physical work?
  ☐ Yes   ☐ No

- Are you persistent and patient?
  ☐ Yes   ☐ No

- Do you have reliable work habits—meaning that once the project is started, will it get finished?
  ☐ Yes   ☐ No

- Do you have all the tools needed and, more importantly, the skills required to do the job?
  ☐ Yes   ☐ No

- Do you have the time that will be required to complete the project? (Always double or triple the time estimated for a DIY project unless you are highly skilled and familiar with that particular project.)
  ☐ Yes   ☐ No

- Will it matter if the project remains unfinished for a period of time?
  ☐ Yes   ☐ No

- Are you prepared to handle the kind of stress this project will create in your family relationships?
  ☐ Yes   ☐ No

- Do you know all of the steps involved in the project?
  ☐ Yes   ☐ No

- Have you gotten the installation instructions from the manufacturer to determine whether this is a project you still want to undertake?
  ☐ Yes      ☐ No

- Is this a job that you can do completely by yourself or will you need assistance?
  ☐ Yes      ☐ No

- Are you familiar with your local building codes and permit requirements? (Some jurisdictions require that the work be completed by a licensed professional in order to meet code. You must check these requirements before beginning work on the project. Additionally, what will you do if the project goes awry? Many contractors are wary about taking on a botched DIY job.)
  ☐ Yes      ☐ No

- Is it safe for you to do this project? (If you are not familiar with roofing, you might not want to venture into a roofing job. Similarly, if you know nothing about electricity—leave it to a professional. Some jobs can be fatal if not performed correctly. Your health and safety should be the primary concern. Never enter into a DIY project that would jeopardize those.)
  ☐ Yes      ☐ No

- Will you be able to obtain the materials you need? (Who will be your source of supply? Will they deliver?)
  ☐ Yes      ☐ No

- Are you attempting to do-it-yourself for financial reasons? If so, have you looked at all of your costs, including the cost of materials, your time, and the tools you need to purchase?
  ☐ Yes      ☐ No

If you answered yes to more than half of these questions, you might attempt a DIY project. But before you run to the nearest hardware store, revisit those questions you marked "No" and carefully consider the potential problems you will face. This quiz is not meant to scare you away from DIY projects. However, you need to be aware that home improvement can be hazardous to your wallet and, more importantly, to your health, if you don't have the skills and aren't properly prepared.

## PICK THE RIGHT HOME IMPROVEMENT PROFESSIONAL

If you are contemplating serving as your own general contractor or hiring a design-build firm, you need to do your homework before signing any contracts. When working with subcontractors, it is cost-effective to get at least three bids for the job. Design-build firms don't work the same way. Because they will be developing the architectural plans for the construction project, they will probably not provide competitive bids.

Here are some questions that NARI recommends that you ask before signing a remodeling contract:

- How long have you been in business?
- Does your company carry Workers' Compensation and liability insurance?
- What is your approach to a project such as this?
- How many projects like mine have you completed in the past year?
- May I have a list of references from those projects?
- May I have a list of business referrals or suppliers?

- What percentage of your business is repeat or referral business?
- Do you belong to any professional organizations or associations in your field? What are they?

Don't take this part lightly. During construction you might spend more time with these professionals than you do with your spouse or partner. You need to like them, trust them, and be able to work with them. In addition to getting answers to the questions above, Hanbury recommends that you also:

- Visit the contractor (unannounced), while he or she is working to see the job site for yourself. Is it relatively clean? Are people actually working or sitting around drinking coffee?
- How is the parking situation? Are there cars parked on the front lawn?
- How loud is the music played by workers?
- How neatly dressed are the workers? Are any of them working without shirts or appropriate footwear?
- Are any of the contractors smoking inside the house?
- Does it look like the contractors are making a good-faith effort to limit damage to the homeowner's property?
- Would you feel comfortable having this contractor at your house? Near your children?

Finding professionals you can work with is crucial. Just because someone comes highly recommended doesn't mean *you* should hire them. You will spend a lot of time with contractors—if you can't get along with them, or feel uncomfortable around them, your job will not be completed to your satisfaction.

Bob Clements says his crews are implored to keep in mind that they are working in someone's home and, if not for the homeowners,

**What Does the Builder See in YOU?** More than just a paycheck, actually. While you are checking out potential builders, they are also evaluating you and your project so they can decide if working with you makes sense for them, too. According to the builders we interviewed, a red flag is raised when their potential customers:

- Don't trust them to do the job.
- Ask them for a professional opinion, then proceed to argue against it.
- Are indecisive about many details.
- Lack a sense of humor.

they wouldn't have a job. But because so many remodelers are swamped with work, some take the attitude that the homeowners are lucky to have them working on their job. Which kind of worker do you want walking through your living room?

Part of the attitude problem might stem from the fact that many qualified building professionals aren't always the best sales or customer service folks, according to builder Carl Seville of Atlanta, Georgia. "Renovating is a series of compromises," he says. Find the right people and put together a team that can work collaboratively to get the job done to your standards, and your home improvement will be successful, says Seville.

Before you hire any builder to touch your home, you must check to ensure that he or she has the current professional licenses and permits to do the necessary work on your home. Ask to see them. Also, check with:

- Your local building department to determine if the town has had any problems with the builder in the past.

- Your state's Better Business Bureau and the Consumer Protection Division of your state's Office of the Attorney General to see if there are any complaints on file against your builder. An Internet search might also turn up some revealing articles about your remodeler or design-build company. (Hopefully they will be accolades about their award-winning work rather than about them skipping town after performing shoddy construction projects.)

We cannot stress enough how important it is to investigate the people who will be working in your home. Vicki received one particularly wrenching e-mail from a Massachusetts woman who had to flee her home because of her poor choice of contractors. When it rained, water dripped from her kitchen light fixture. The walls and ceilings began to crack. The entire attic was infested with slimy mold.

It happened like this: She and her husband hired a contractor to replace the roof on their home. His estimate was low and the couple was thrilled to save money on the repair. They asked the contractor if he was licensed and insured. He assured them he was. (They didn't ask for proof, however.) The contractor quickly ripped off the roof, but was incredibly slow to replace it. In the meantime, it began to rain and the home was left open to the elements. When the contractor routinely failed to show up for work, the woman began to investigate, using the sources noted above. She was horrified to find out that he did *not* have a contractor's license or insurance.

Yes, it gets worse. The reason why this contractor missed so many days of work was that he was a defendant in a child pornography case being tried in a courtroom a few towns over. Unbeknownst to the homeowners, he was sitting in front of a judge and jury on days he was supposed to be shingling their roof. Sadly, this couple learned an expensive lesson. Instead of increasing the value of their home, this contractor rendered their home worthless. It had to be gutted. As for recompense for the owners? There was none. The state could do nothing, citing the old adage: "Buyer beware." The homeowners' only option was to sue the contractor. However, the couple didn't pursue a lawsuit because they learned from their attorney that the contractor had spent all his money defending himself against the child pornography charges, was found guilty, and sentenced to jail.

If you still have any doubts about how widespread the problem is within the building and remodeling industries, take a moment and visit Homeowners Against Deficient Dwellings (HADD) at *www.hadd.com*. The nonprofit group was founded to promote better building standards and practices, to educate the general public how to avoid substandard, deficient housing, and to rectify current instances of substandard, deficient housing. The homeowners' stories serve as cautionary tales for anyone who is about to embark on a home improvement project that requires hiring building professionals.

## GET IT ALL IN WRITING

Unless you are serving as your own general contractor, you should get all the details of your home improvement project in writing. This will help you avoid problems, or at least provide documentation if you encounter them. The more details you outline, the less chance there will be of a misunderstanding between you and your contractor after the project is underway.

You must communicate openly with all the professionals working on your home and clearly spell out your expectations. Make sure that your home improvement contract covers:

- Specific materials need to complete the job.
- The project start date.
- The project end date.
- Specific project notations, written on the plans by the architect, and agreed upon and initialed by the builder and/or each subcontractor.

- Cleanup rules.
- Hours of work.
- A warranty that addresses materials and workmanship.

# A WORD ABOUT COSTS

Nobody wants to spend more on home improvements than they have to, but it's important to keep in mind that the lowest price doesn't necessarily equal the best value. If you are at all concerned about the resale value of your home and its improvements, your projects must be done right.

By all means, shop around. But make sure you get an apples-to-apples price comparison, otherwise the numbers will be meaningless. Every project detail must match—from the materials quoted, to the length of time it will take to complete the job, to cleanup estimates. (Rental dumpsters don't come cheap.)

Often the difference between two contractors of similar skills is the "allowance" that they quote you on your project. For example, one contractor might budget the least expensive bathroom fixtures to keep his bid as low as possible, while the other contractor quotes you a price that includes high-end fixtures. Depending on the size of the project, the differences in the allowances can run from a couple hundred to thousands of dollars.

If you have the time, energy, and talent to do the job yourself, you *will* spend less money. However, if you don't have the necessary remodeling skills, you start the project, and then have to call someone to bail you out, then you won't save a dime. In fact, your home improvement might cost more money in the long run than if you had just hired a professional in the first place.

You can also save money if you know good subcontractors who are willing to give you high-quality work for a reasonable price and you are prepared to serve as your own general contractor. On the other hand, some design-build firms can meet or exceed their competitors' quotes by reconfiguring the space you're planning on improving. Another possible advantage of hiring a design-build firm is that their architectural fees are often substantially lower than those paid to independent architects.

One last variable to consider in your pricing equation: Quality design-build firms supply a uniform professional touch to your job that is difficult to achieve when parts of your home improvement are parceled out piecemeal to subcontractors, or you're designing the project yourself. The outcome might very well be the difference between a reaction of, "Nice," versus, "WOW!" from your family and friends when you reveal your completed project.

# CHAPTER 10

# KEEP YOUR HOME IMPROVEMENT PROJECT ON TRACK

# WHY DO GOOD PROJECTS GO BAD?

Time and money. These are the two crucial elements required for any successful home improvement project. They're also the two elements that cause homeowners the most grief during remodeling. It's a given that once your project schedule goes off track, so does your budget. If you want to maximize the value of your home, you're not going to do it by planning a $30,000 kitchen remodel that winds up costing you $50,000 due to delays and worker no-shows.

Home improvement schedules derail for two main reasons:

- The contractor (or subcontractors) don't show up on time—or worse, they come for a day and then don't return for a week, or more!

- The project materials aren't ready for the workers because you didn't select and order them far enough in advance.

The first problem—getting contractors and subcontractors on your job and keeping them there—can be extremely frustrating. But there are several steps you can take to avoid this situation. For starters, review the criteria for selecting home improvement professionals in Chapter 9. Next, establish clear communication with the professionals who will be working in your home. Additionally, make sure each worker can perform his or her job without endlessly waiting around for others to finish theirs. For example, if the framer isn't finished, don't schedule the electrician to come in and begin roughing in electrical wiring for your addition.

Equally important to clearly communicating with the workers is how you treat them. If you're serving as general contractor, make sure

> **TIP:** *Builder Bob Clements suggests that homeowners buy a clipboard and use it to jot down their project questions and concerns on a daily basis. Then the contractor (or subcontractors) can review the clipboard each morning and respond appropriately. This will reduce the number of phone calls to the builder's office and cut down on the frustration of playing telephone tag.*

your worksite is 100-percent ready when they arrive each morning. If they show up and you don't have the necessary permits or all the materials you promised, don't be surprised when they leave and don't return for another two weeks. Clear up any outstanding issues well in advance of their arrival. Find out how they want to be paid and pay them on time. Remember that this is how they support their families and pay their employees. They're professionals whose time is every bit as valuable as yours is—so treat them that way.

> **TIP:** *When you find quality craftsmen, treat them like family, refer them to everyone you know, and pay them promptly. Good manners and respect never go out of style. You'll be glad you made the effort when you need to rehire them for your next job.*

# ORDER MATERIALS ASAP

It's absolutely crucial that you select and order essential project materials well before the project's start date. You might end up with a garage full of 2-x-4s for days, weeks, or even months ahead of time. But what's worse? Your contractor showing up, eager to work, and you have to send him on his way because you're still waiting for the lumber to arrive.

Additionally, you want to order early so you can avoid any rush orders. These are always more costly and can result in mistakes leading to yet more expense and scheduling problems.

Items you need to order well in advance include:

- **Windows.** Without windows, your home addition will grind to a halt, and reordering can easily take four to six weeks. Yes, your contractor can dig and pour the foundation, frame it, and even put a roof over it, but siding will be delayed, as well as all the finish work inside.

- **Cabinets.** It might take four to six weeks to order stock cabinets, but popular models and custom-designed cabinetry can take up to six *months.* Popular models sometimes have a waiting list, and lumber shortages, labor disputes, and factory service interruptions are all possible, so plan ahead!

- **Heating and cooling hardware.** Remodeling often means working with heating and cooling systems for which it can be difficult to get parts. For example, Dan's house has steam heat. He can't just run out to the plumbing supply store and pick up a four-foot steam convector. Parts such as these can take inordinate amounts of time to locate and order.

- **Countertops.** Because your choices for countertops are virtually limitless, you need to start shopping well in advance of when you will need them.

- **Flooring.** Tile, specialty woods, and rugs can all take an incredible amount of time to select. Tile alone can take weeks to pick out because there's a rainbow of stock and custom colors and thousands of different tile sizes, textures, and highlight pieces available. As for rugs, some take two weeks to arrive from the order date; others take two months. Care to guess how long yours will take to arrive if you wait until the last minute? Order as soon as possible.

- Molding. Stock molding doesn't take long to get. However, if you choose nonstandard molding, it will take longer. And, if you live in a part of the country where builders are frantically busy, getting a fabricator to assemble the molding for your doors and windows can set you back 6 to 12 weeks.

Remember that spot shortages of building materials do occur. Framing lumber, plywood, and sheetrock—all materials that are usually readily available—can occasionally fall into short supply, particularly after a natural disaster, such as a wildfire, flood, tornado, or hurricane. To ensure that you don't get caught by surprise, stay in touch with your contractor or your local home improvement store if you are doing the work yourself.

## CONTROL COSTS

OK, the materials have all arrived and you have the workers all lined up. You still need to keep a wary eye on your project budget, even after the first nail is hammered. Limit the "while you are here, you might as well" additions to your home improvement. It's easy to get carried away when you see quality new craftsmanship right next to a room that hasn't been changed since it was built 50 years ago.

Sometimes it makes economic sense to add to the project while subcontractors are in your house—perhaps upgrading the electrical service or fixing some leaky plumbing—but remember, it's going to mess with your carefully planned budget. After months of mapping out your home improvement, don't make any snap decisions just because the builder is standing next to you. Better to halt work for a day and give yourself a night to mull over a new direction and run the numbers than to just say "Go ahead," and then have to worry about how you're going to scrape up another $10,000.

But as long as you have done your planning, hired quality craftsmen, and the work is smoothly progressing, don't panic halfway through the project and stop construction. For instance, Dan's master bedroom addition included one 36-by-52-inch window on one side of the room and two similar-sized windows mulled together in the front of his house. When the front of the addition was framed, the gaping space for those windows looked huge! Dan and Janet nearly panicked and stopped construction. They thought they would never have any privacy in that room unless the blinds were drawn. Their builder calmed their nerves and the project went on. Now, with the room finished and the curtains up, it's amazing to see how much smaller those windows look.

The moral to this story? Listen to the experts that you hired! If you've done your job properly—by screening the professionals who are working in your home—trust them to do their job. This doesn't mean that you can't question any of their actions or decisions, but do give credence to their references and examples of their quality craftsmanship.

## IT AIN'T OVER 'TIL *YOU* SAY SO

Your home improvement is not finished until you say it is. It's that simple. You should never say it is finished (and deliver the final payment) until you have gone over your improvement with a fine-tooth comb. Items can and do get overlooked. To maximize the return on your investment, you need to hold the contractor and subcontractors to the specifications you all agreed upon when you signed the contracts.

When it comes to the finished project, building inspectors can be your best friends. Their job is to make sure your addition is up to code, and that all systems work properly, including plumbing and electrical. That doesn't mean that all building inspectors are created equal—far from it. Just as you selected your contractor carefully, if your municipality has more than one inspector, you might want to try to work with the one that has the reputation for being the most thorough and fair.

During one of Dan's many remodeling projects, a building inspector came in quite handy when he found some leaky plumbing that Dan hadn't noticed and wouldn't have discovered until the walls were closed in and the job was done. Remember, if your addition isn't completed in a quality manner, the desirability of your home might be reduced, and your return on your investment will be lower.

Before you make the final payment for your home improvement, use this checklist to review the job and ensure that the work is completed to your original specifications.

- Check all plugs and switches to ensure that they are working properly.
- Check all plumbing for leaks and drips. Don't just let the water run for 30 seconds! Run full blast for at least five minutes.
- Flush the toilet several times in succession.
- Look at your walls on an angle at night with a dim light that casts shadows to find any noticeable nail or screw pops and other imperfections.
- Turn on the heat to make sure it works and isn't overly noisy, even if it's 90 degrees outside.
- Turn on the air conditioning to make sure it works and isn't overly noisy, even if it's 10 degrees outside.
- Check out all mechanicals, including appliances, bubble tubs, and fireplaces. (Is the refrigerator balanced so the door closes on its own?)
- Did the painters miss any spots? Did they drip paint? Did they leave you with touch-up paint? (If they didn't, ask them for some.)

## LESSONS LEARNED: RECORDKEEPING

Your first home improvement will not be your last. It's important to learn from the mistakes that you made the first time around so that you don't repeat them. One of the best ways to do this is to keep good notes during your project. Documentation serves many purposes. If a snafu occurs during the project, you will have a written record. (If you should have to sue your contractor, you will have a dated journal of how the events unfolded.) After the project is over, these notes will help you to identify which contractors you will hire again—and those you won't.

But the most important reason to keep good records is that your house, like most, will eventually be sold. When it does sell, there might be tax consequences.

There are special tax exclusions that apply to the sale of a home used as a principal residence. Generally speaking, you may exclude up to $250,000 of gain ($500,000 if filing a joint return) on the sale of such a home. (Losses on the sale are *not* tax deductible.) To benefit from the exclusion, you must meet certain ownership and use tests and you can't use the exclusion more than once every two years.

To minimize, or even eliminate, paying taxes on the sale of your principal residence, you must keep accurate records in order to calculate the gain or loss that is realized on the sale. The gain or loss is calculated by subtracting the adjusted basis (the original purchase price plus permanent improvements) from the sales price (gross sales price less selling expenses) of the home.

For example, let's say you purchased your home in 1985 for $160,000. In 1986, you put on a new roof for $4000. In 1998, you installed a brick patio for $6000. In 1990, you remodeled the kitchen for $40,000. In 1995, you added on a family room for $50,000. If you add those improvements to your original purchase price, that increases your adjusted basis to $260,000 ($160,000 for the original purchase price plus $100,000 for improvements).

Now let's say you sell this house today for $313,000 and pay a $3000 commission to the real estate agent. Subtract the commission from the gross sales price and your net sales price is $310,000. From $310,000, subtract your adjusted basis ($260,000), and your gain is $50,000. Without accurate records, you can't prove your $100,000 investment in home improvements. This would increase your $50,000 gain by two-thirds, to $150,000!

Here are examples of permanent home improvements that increase the value of your home and may be added to your basis:

- Additions of any kind.
- Landscaping, such as plants, walkways, fencing, sprinkler systems, swimming pools, decks, and patios.
- Plumbing such as water heaters, septic systems, wells and water filtration systems, heating and air conditioning systems.
- Remodeling, such as new windows and doors, new roof, wiring upgrades, security system, satellite dish, kitchens, wall-to-wall carpeting, flooring, and insulation.

However, there are a few items that *reduce* your basis. They include any improvements that are no longer part of your home, such as removal of carpeting, flooring, or fencing, and any gain you postponed from the sale of a previous home prior to May 7, 1997. Also, routine maintenance of your home, such as painting and repairs, does not generally increase the basis of your home.

The $250,000/$500,000 gain exclusion minimizes the need for accurate records in many cases because there are no tax consequences. However, there are some situations where you could end up having to pay taxes, including:

- You intend to live, or have lived, in your home a long time.
- Your home is rapidly appreciating in value.
- You decide to take a depreciation deduction for home office use or rental of your home. The depreciated portion of your home may not qualify for the exclusion.

If you're unsure about the rules (and Dan's wife Janet, the CPA, tells us that they're quite complicated) consult your tax advisor. Even though you might not end up paying any taxes, you must be able to prove you qualify for the exclusion and prove your gain is below the $250,000 or $500,000 threshold. It is important to remember that if you've rented your home or taken depreciation on it, a portion of the gain may not qualify for the exclusion. For more detail, see Internal Revenue Service Publication 523, *Selling Your Home*, located at *www.irs.gov*.

# PART 4

# GIMME SHELTER: PROTECT YOUR INVESTMENT

# CHAPTER 11

# PROPER MAINTENANCE FOR A SAFER, MORE VALUABLE HOME

# BUDGET FOR UPKEEP AND REPAIRS

You've just spent $35,000 to update your kitchen and add a small bathroom. To pay for it, you took out a home equity loan that costs you a couple hundred extra dollars per month. Now think about your other monthly expenses for just a minute. (Believe us, we have to force ourselves to do this exercise, too.)

There's the mortgage and payments for your car, fuel, electricity, food, clothing, insurance, daycare, cable television, Internet access, telephone, cell phones, and pet supplies. But there's another monthly budget item that *should* be included in every homeowner's list, but rarely is—the cash you set aside each month for home maintenance and repairs.

Home experts recommend that you set aside a little money each month (between one and three percent of the value of your home annually) to prevent what should be manageable home upkeep and repairs from turning into hellish home defects. If you forgo this ounce of prevention, your pound of cure might very well swallow not only your $35,000 remodeling investment, but the *entire* value of your home, potentially leaving you on the brink of bankruptcy and homelessness.

Could that really happen, you ask? Unfortunately the answer is this: quite easily. All it takes is one arcing spark from faulty wiring and a basement full of old newspapers and your investment is gone up in smoke. A leaky roof left unrepaired can result in an attic full of mold. Vicki's inbox at *vicki@moldauthor.com* is crammed with e-mail from folks struggling to cope with the financial, physical, and emotional devastation wreaked on them by severe mold infestations that are the direct result of improper home maintenance and repairs, construction defects, or faulty home inspections.

But the losses don't have to be this dramatic to hurt your bottom line. Those granite countertops in your kitchen aren't going to sway a potential homebuyer into offering you your full asking price if the cabinets underneath them are sporting broken or missing hardware and cracked or peeling paint. Deferred maintenance (even in only one or two places) shout neglect. Depending on their nature and location, undone repairs can lop off $10,000 to $20,000 (or more) from the offers you receive on your home.

The following tips can help keep your home properly maintained to ensure that your home's value isn't reduced.

# TIPS TO PREVENT DAMAGE FROM FIRE AND LIGHTNING

The residential property damage from fires and lightning each year is enormous. According to the National Fire Protection Agency, there were 389,000 reported home fires in the United States in 2002, resulting in 2670 deaths, 13,650 injuries, and $5.9 billion in direct property damage. In addition, electrical storms cause approximately $100 million dollars annually in property damage, according to the Federal Emergency Management Agency. While smoking is the leading cause of home fire deaths overall, cooking is the leading cause of home fires and home fire injuries year-round.

To protect yourself, your family, and your home from fire and the effects of lightning, you should:

- Keep a fire extinguisher in an accessible spot.
- Install electrical power surge strips.
- Trip and reset circuit breakers to make sure they're functioning properly.
- Inspect electrical power and extension cords for signs of wear or damage.
- Inspect and clean dirt from the covers of all smoke and carbon monoxide detectors. (Replace the batteries annually.)

- Clean the grease and grime from stove hoods and stove exhaust fans to prevent a cooking fire from spreading.

- Check for loose-fitting plugs. This is often a sign that the electrical receptacle is worn.

- Inspect your home's main electrical panel for burn marks. These marks might indicate "arcing" inside the panel, which can spark a fire. If you see evidence of arcing, call an electrician. Only a qualified professional should remove the front panel cover. Additionally, do not stack newspapers, magazines, or cardboard boxes near electrical sources.

- Make sure the light bulbs in all your fixtures are the correct wattage. Incorrect wattage leads to heat buildup that can start a fire inside the fixture, the ceiling, or the wall.

- If you use fireplaces, wood stoves, or electric heaters, watch them closely and make sure they are working properly. Have your chimney professionally cleaned at least once a year.

## TIPS TO PREVENT DAMAGE FROM WIND AND HAIL

According to the Insurance Information Institute, homeowners' losses due to wind and hail totaled $4.2 billion in 2000. This figure highlights the fact that wind and hail rank among the top five causes of property loss in the nation. Particularly susceptible are homes with deficient roofing and siding. To protect yourself, your family, and your home from wind and hail damage, you should:

- Check your roof for problems and replace damaged or missing shingles.

- Replace the entire roof when warranted. Although the actual life span of your roof is determined by many factors (including climate, environmental conditions, and the quality of the roofing material and its installation), you should put on a new roof if it is more than 20 years old and the shingles are cracking and/or curling. Additionally, you should reroof if it is more than 15 years old and you're noticing leaks in more than one area.

- When replacing your roof, make sure the new shingles have a Class 4 rating under the Underwriters Laboratories' (UL) 2218 standard. A Class 4 rating means that a sample of the product did not crack when hit twice in the same area by a two-inch steel ball.

- Keep trees and shrubbery trimmed. Remove diseased or damaged limbs.

- Inspect lightweight vinyl or aluminum siding for wear and tear. Wind can catch loose seams and corners and tear the siding off the walls.

- Remove any debris or loose items from your yard well in advance of an approaching storm. Put away lawn furniture and patio umbrellas. Secure firewood. Close window shutters.

## TIPS TO PREVENT WATER DAMAGE

Gone are the days when you might ignore a damp basement or a mildly leaking faucet. That's because today's informed homeowners know that water damage is not only an invitation to mold, but to dry rot and pest infestation as well. The havoc wreaked by a "water event"—from a leaky basement to a frozen and ruptured water pipe—can also ultimately lead to the nonrenewal of your home insurance, or even a lawsuit. (Don't even *think* about selling your home without first disclosing water or mold problems. For more information, see "Making Claims: You Better Get a CLUE" in Chapter 12.)

Damage due to water and freezing temperatures caused home-owners losses totaling $4.96 billion in 2000, according to the Insurance Information Institute. This is one of the reasons home insurance has risen an average of 5 to 8 percent in the past few years. To protect yourself, your family, and your home from water damage and the effects of frigid temperatures, you should:

- Fix any leaks immediately. For added protection, install a leak detector. Ask your insurance agent if this qualifies you for a discount on your home insurance.
- Keep downspouts and gutters clean to prevent water or ice from building up on your roof.
- Insulate all pipes that are susceptible to freezing.
- Set your home's thermostat no lower than 55 degrees.
- Inspect all windows, exterior doors, trim, and flashing for signs of damage.

> **TIP:** *Routinely check your home's water pressure. The ideal pressure is somewhere in the range of 60 to 80 pounds per square inch. Anything above this has the potential to wear out the washers in your faucets and cause a leak. You can check your water pressure by purchasing a water pressure gauge at a local home improvement center. To determine water pressure, attach the gauge to an outdoor faucet and turn water on full to determine the pressure. Make adjustments as necessary or contact a plumber to adjust it for you.*

- Check the water hoses on your washing machine, refrigerator icemaker, and dishwasher for signs of wear.
- Check your water heater for leaks. Partially drain the heater every six months to prevent sediment from building up on the bottom.
- Check shutoff valves at each plumbing fixture for signs of leaks. Shut off the valve for your washing machine after each use.
- Check for cracked or missing grout around the base of your toilet, bathtub and/or shower, and bathroom cabinets.

- Keep the humidity in your home and basement less than 50 percent. You can check by using an inexpensive hygrometer, an instrument that measures the water vapor content of the air. (You can find hygrometers in some home improvement stores and on the Internet.)
- Make sure bathrooms and kitchens are well vented.
- Prevent vines from growing on your house.
- Don't stack firewood near your house.
- Make sure lawn sprinklers do not constantly wet one area of your house.
- Paint any exposed wood surfaces to prevent them from decaying.

## TIPS TO PREVENT PERSONAL INJURIES

You call it "Home Sweet Home"—that place you go to at the end of the day to unwind and relax—a haven where you shelter yourself and your loved ones from an increasingly chaotic and dangerous world. But the reality is somewhat different. In American homes each year, there is a fatal injury about every 16 minutes and a disabling injury every 4 seconds, according to the American Safety Council. The four leading fatal events are poisonings, falls, fires and burns, and suffocation by an ingested object. The leading cause of death in the home, poisoning, took the lives of 12,500 people in 2002. The 25 to 44 age group had the highest death rate. Falls—the second leading cause of home deaths—took the lives of 8000 people, 4 out of 5 of them over the age of 65.

Deaths and injuries in the home exact a terrible emotional and financial toll. Each year, people make home insurance claims totaling more than $900 million. Worse, personal injury or wrongful death lawsuits filed against these homeowners can, and do, result in several-hundred-thousand-dollar judgments against them. While most liability lawsuits are settled out of court, it only takes one successful lawsuit to wreak havoc on you and your family. Even if the lawsuit doesn't make it to court, the emotional turmoil and financial hardship of defending yourself can leave you exhausted and can easily result in bankruptcy or the loss of your home and other valuable personal assets. This is one area where you just can't afford to go uninformed—or underinsured. (For more information, see Chapter 12.)

To protect yourself, your family, and your home from injury and liability losses, you should:

- Repair all cracked, broken, or uneven driveways and walks to help provide a level walking surface.

- Replace broken stair treads. Painted wood or concrete stairs can be slippery when wet or when a person's shoes are wet. Resurface the treads with slip-resistant strips near the stair nosing. All stairs with at least three risers should have a handrail.

- Make sure stairs and stairwells are adequately lit, particularly at night.

- Scatter rugs can be extremely dangerous, especially with young children and/or the elderly in your home. Make sure all scatter rugs have a skid-resistant backing or pad beneath them.

- Keep clutter to a minimum. Make sure lamp and other electrical cords are kept away from foot traffic.

- Keep all prescription and over-the-counter medicines in their original packaging. Don't store prescription drugs or over-the-counter medicines in an unlocked bathroom or kitchen cabinet. If you have children in your home, don't store bleach or other cleaning materials in under-the-counter cabinets without child-safety latches.

- Socialize your dog to help reduce potential dog bites. According to the Centers for Disease Control and Prevention, there are approximately 4.7 million dog bites per year. These bites cost over $1 billion, with the property/casualty insurance industry paying roughly $310 million in 2001, accounting for 1/3 of the total number of homeowners' insurance liability claims.

- Never use a trampoline without a spotter. Children must have adult supervision at all times. Somersaults are the leading cause of quadriplegic injuries and should never be permitted. Nearly 250,000 people are hurt each year in trampoline accidents, according to the Insurance Information Institute (III).

- Make sure there is secure fencing around any pool to keep children and unauthorized individuals from the pool area. All gates should be self-closing. Keep gates locked when pool is not in use. Pool slides and diving boards can be extremely dangerous. Consider removing them. Never swim alone and do not let children swim without adult supervision. The III says more than 600 people drown in pools annually and another 43,000 are injured in and around them.

- Store guns, unloaded, in a place that is inaccessible to children. Keep the ammunition in a separate location under lock and key. Educate your family about gun safety. Currently, 18 states (California, Connecticut, Delaware, Florida, Hawaii, Illinois, Iowa, Maryland, Massachusetts, Minnesota, Nevada, New Hampshire, New Jersey, North Carolina, Rhode Island, Texas, Virginia, and Wisconsin) have enacted "Child Access Prevention" (CAP) laws. These laws dictate that when a child obtains an improperly stored, loaded gun, the adult owner is civilly and criminally liable.

- Don't store dirty, oily rags in your garage or shed. Run all gas-powered lawn equipment and grills until the fuel tanks are empty before you store them for the winter. **Note:** Use caution when using such outdoor equipment. Each year, 75 people are killed and about 200,000 are injured on or near riding lawnmowers and garden tractors. One out of every five deaths involves a child who

**Gun stun:** In a nationwide survey of 806 parents, 43 percent of households with children have guns, according to the Brady Campaign to Prevent Gun Violence. Of those homes, 1 in 10 has a loaded gun, and 1 in 8 has a gun that is unlocked and "hidden away." While 54 percent of the parents surveyed said they would be "highly concerned" if they knew there was a gun in the home of their child's friend, 61 percent said they never thought about asking other parents about gun accessibility. Only 30 percent said they have asked the parents of their children's friends if there is a gun in the home before allowing a visit.

was in the path of a moving mower. Additionally, every year gas and charcoal grills cause an average of 1500 structure fires and 4800 outdoor fires in or on home properties, according to the National Fire Protection Association.

- Routinely inspect swing sets, slides, porch swings, gliders, jungle gyms, and play-scapes for signs of wear. Go over safety rules with your family. Of the approximately 156,000 playground-equipment-related injuries that occur each year, 46,930 (nearly 23 percent) occur on equipment designed for home use.

While much of this is common sense, it is crucial to remember that proper home maintenance will do as much to maximize the value of your home as the improvement projects mentioned in this book. Additionally, proper home safety will help you avoid a liability lawsuit that could potentially devastate you both emotionally and financially.

# CHAPTER 12

# INSURANCE: PROTECT YOUR INVESTMENT

# HOW MUCH HOME INSURANCE DO YOU NEED?

After you have spent the time and money to increase the value of your home, you must take steps to protect that investment. You need insurance.

There's no way around it: If you owe the bank for your home, then you must pony up for home insurance. You can't get a mortgage without it. Some banks require you to buy home insurance to cover the amount of your mortgage. But if the limit of your home insurance policy is based on your mortgage, make sure it's enough to cover the cost of rebuilding if a disaster strikes your home. Additionally, if your mortgage is paid off, don't cancel your policy! Home insurance protects your investment in your home.

So when *was* the last time you took a good look at your policy? If the answer is "years," then your policy needs updating. Have you added an extra room? Put in a pool? Installed a new security system? All of these can have a big impact on your home insurance. According to the Insurance Information Institute, you need enough insurance to cover:

- *The structure.* You should adjust your home insurance whenever you remodel. You need enough home insurance to cover the cost of rebuilding your improved home at *current* construction costs. Remember, your amended policy should reflect your home's *new* net worth.

  For a quick estimate of the amount of insurance you need, multiply the total square footage of your home by local building costs per square foot. You can find out these costs by doing a little investigative work. Call a local real estate agent or builder. You can also ask an insurance agent who does business in your neighborhood.

Most standard home insurance policies will pay to repair or rebuild your home if it is damaged or destroyed by fire, hurricane, hail, lightning, or other disaster listed in your policy. It will not pay for damage caused by a flood, earthquake, or routine wear and tear. Standard policies also cover structures that are detached from your home, such as a garage, tool shed, or gazebo. Generally, these structures are covered for about 10 percent of the amount of insurance you have on the structure of your home. If you need more coverage, speak with your insurance agent about purchasing more insurance.

- *Your personal possessions.* Your furniture, clothes, sports equipment, and other personal items are covered if they are stolen or destroyed by fire, hurricane, or other insured disaster. Most home insurers provide coverage for 40 percent to 70 percent of the amount of insurance you have on the structure or "dwelling" of your home. For example, if you have $100,000 worth of insurance on the structure of your home, you would have between $40,000

---

### OTHER FACTORS THAT DETERMINE THE COST OF REBUILDING YOUR HOME

- The type of exterior wall construction (frame, masonry, or veneer).
- The style of the house (ranch, colonial, cape, split-level).
- The number of rooms (especially bathrooms).
- Other structures on the premises such as garages and sheds.
- Fireplaces, exterior trim, and other special features such as arched windows.
- Whether the house (or parts of it) were custom built.

Source: Insurance Information Institute

---

and $70,000 worth of coverage for your belongings. The limits of the policy typically appear on the *Declarations Page* under *Section I, Coverages, A. Dwelling.* To determine if this is enough coverage, you need to conduct a home inventory. This is a detailed list of everything you own and information related to the cost to replace these items if they were stolen or destroyed. Your inventory should list each item, its value, and serial number. Photograph or videotape each room, including closets, open drawers, storage buildings, and your garage. Keep receipts for major items in a fireproof place. If you think you need more coverage, contact your agent or insurer and ask for higher limits for your personal possessions.

Additionally, there might be a limit on how much you get for expensive items such as jewelry and silverware. Generally, there is limit on jewelry of $1000 to $2000.

This information is in *Section I, Personal Property, Special Limits of Liability.* Insurers might also place a limit on what they'll pay for computers. If the limits are too low, consider

---

**Replacement cost versus actual cash value.** You can insure your possessions in two ways: For their *actual cash value* or for their *replacement cost.* A cash value policy pays the cost to replace your belongings minus depreciation. A replacement cost policy, on the other hand, reimburses you for the actual current cost to replace the item.

For example, a fire destroys a 10-year-old television in your living room. If you have a replacement cost policy for the contents of your home, the insurer will pay to replace the TV set with a new one. If you have an actual cash policy, it will pay only a percentage of the cost of a new TV set because the TV has been used for 10 years and is worth a lot less than the original.

Source: Insurance Information Institute

---

**Supplemental Coverage.** Depending on where you live, you might need to supplement your policy with special coverage. Home insurance policies don't cover damage caused by floods or earthquakes. The National Flood Insurance Program (NFIP) offers flood coverage in many areas. For more information, call NFIP at (800) 427-4661.

In California, the California Earthquake Authority (CEA) offers basic earthquake insurance for California homeowners, renters, condominium owners, and mobile home owners. You can call CEA toll-free at (877) 797-4300.

buying a special personal property floater or an endorsement. These allow you to insure these times individually or as a collection. With floaters and endorsements, there is no deductible. You are charged a premium based on what the item (or collection) is, where you live, and its dollar value. You can determine the value by providing your agent with a return receipt or getting the item or collection appraised.

Trees, plants, and shrubs are also covered under a standard home insurance policy. Generally you are covered for five percent of the insurance on the house, up to about $500 per item. Perils covered are theft, fire, lightning, explosion, vandalism, riot, and even falling aircraft. They are not covered for damage by wind or disease.

• *Additional living expenses* (ALE) *after a disaster.* This is a very important feature of a standard home insurance policy. This pays the additional costs of temporarily living away from your home due to a fire, severe storm, or other disaster. It covers hotel bills, restaurant meals, and other living expenses incurred while your home is being rebuilt.

Coverage for additional living expenses differs from insurer to insurer. Many policies provide coverage for about

20 percent of the insurance on your house. If you rent out part of your house, this coverage also reimburses you for the rent that you would have collected from your tenant if your home had not been destroyed.

- *Liability to others.* Liability insurance protects your assets in case you are sued for bodily injury or property damage that you or family members cause to other people. It also pays for damage to others caused by your pets. (If your dog accidentally slips into your neighbors' house and chews up their Oriental rug, you're covered. However, if your dog destroys your own rug, you're not covered.) Additionally, your home insurance policy also provides no-fault medical coverage.

  In the event that a friend or neighbor is injured in your home, he or she can simply submit the medical bills to your insurer. This way, expenses are paid without the injured person filing a liability claim against you. You can generally buy $1000 to $5000 worth of this coverage. However, it does not pay the medical bills for you, your family, or your pet.

  Liability limits generally start at $100,000. However, most experts recommend that you purchase at least $300,000 worth of protection. If you own property or have investments and savings that are worth more than the liability limits in your policy, you should consider purchasing excess liability insurance, also known as an "umbrella" policy.

## WHAT IS AN UMBRELLA POLICY AND WHEN DO YOU NEED ONE?

Umbrella policies start to pay after you have exhausted the liability insurance in your underlying home (or auto) policy. An umbrella policy isn't part of your home insurance policy. You must purchase it separately. The cost of an umbrella policy depends on how much underlying insurance you have and the kind of risk you represent. The greater the amount of underlying coverage you have, the cheaper the policy. This is because you would be less likely to need the additional insurance. Most insurers require a minimum of $300,000 on your home and your car before they will issue you an umbrella policy.

An umbrella policy provides much broader coverage than your standard home insurance policy, including protection for claims against you for libel and slander and invasion of privacy. These are not covered under standard home insurance policies. Generally, umbrella policies cost between $200 to $350 for $1 million worth of coverage.

## THE TOP 10 WAYS TO SAVE MONEY ON YOUR HOME INSURANCE

Your insurer decides what to charge you for home insurance based on many factors. Is your home equipped with a security system, smoke detectors, and deadbolt locks? If so, then you could save money because these items help make your home safer and more secure. Do you have an in-ground pool or a trampoline? If so, then you will pay higher premiums than a homeowner who doesn't. You can also expect to pay more if you are located in a higher risk area, such as a coastline that is susceptible to storms and flooding. Your insurer will also want to know if you plan to use your home for any business purposes, or if you plan to rent all or part of the house, both of which can increase liability.

The price you pay for your home insurance can vary by hundreds of dollars, depending on the size of your house, its location, and the insurer you buy your policy from. According to the Insurance Information Institute, here are 10 ways to save money on your home insurance policy:

1. *Shop around.* Prices vary from company to company, so it pays to go shopping. Get at least three price quotes. You can call companies directly or access information on the Internet.

**TIP:** *Don't shop on price alone. You want an insurer that answers your questions and handles claims fairly and efficiently. Ask friends and relatives for their recommendations. Contact your state insurance department to find out whether they make available consumer complaint ratios by insurer. Select an agent or company representative that takes the time to answer your questions. Remember, you'll be dealing with this company if you have an accident or other emergency.*

Your state insurance department might also provide comparisons of prices charged by major insurers. You buy insurance to protect yourself financially and provide peace of mind, so it's important to pick a company that is financially stable. Check the financial health of insurers with rating companies such as A.M. Best ( *http://www.ambest.com*) and Standard & Poor's (*http://www.standardandpoors.com/ratings*) and consult consumer magazines.

Get quotes from different types of insurers. Some sell through their own agents. These agencies have the same name as the insurance company. Some sell through independent agents who offer policies from several insurers. Others don't use agents. They sell directly to consumers over the phone or via the Internet.

2. *Raise your deductible.* A deductible is the amount of money you have to pay toward a loss before your insurer starts to pay a claim. The higher your deductible, the more money you save on your premium. Consider a deductible of at least $500. If you can afford to raise it to $1000, you might save as much as 25 percent.

If you live in a disaster-prone area, your insurance policy might have a separate deductible for damage from major disasters. If you live near the East Coast, you might have a separate windstorm deductible. If you live in a state vulnerable to hail storms, you might have a separate deductible for hail. If you live in an earthquake-prone area, your earthquake policy has a deductible.

3. *Buy your home and auto policies from the same insurer.* Most companies that sell home insurance also sell auto and umbrella liability insurance. Some insurers will reduce your premium by 5 percent to 15 percent if you buy two or more insurance policies from them. But make certain that this combined price is lower than buying coverage from different companies.

4. *Make your home more disaster resistant.* Find out from your insurance agent or company representative what you can do to make your home more resistant to windstorms and other natural disasters. You might be able to save on your premiums by adding storm shutters and shatterproof glass, reinforcing your roof, or buying stronger roofing materials. Older homes can be retrofitted to make them better able to withstand earthquakes. In addition, consider modernizing your heating, plumbing, and electrical systems to reduce the risk of fire and water damage.

5. *Don't confuse what you paid for your house with rebuilding costs.* The land under your house isn't at risk from theft, windstorm, fire, and the other perils covered in your homeowner's policy. So don't include its value in deciding how much homeowner's insurance to buy. If you do, you'll pay a higher premium than you should.

6. *Ask about discounts for home security devices.* You can usually get discounts of at least 5 percent for a smoke detector, burglar alarm, or dead-bolt locks. Some insurers might cut your premiums by as much as 20 percent if you install a sophisticated sprinkler system and a fire and burglar alarm that rings at the police, fire, or other monitoring stations. These systems aren't cheap and not every system qualifies for a discount.

Before you buy one, find out what kind your insurer recommends, how much the device would cost, and how much you'd save on premiums.

7. *Seek out other discounts.* Many companies offer discounts, but they don't all offer the same discount or the same amount of discount in all states. Ask your agent or company representative about discounts available to you. For example, if you're at least 55 years old and retired, you might qualify for a discount of up to 10 percent at some companies. If you've completely modernized your plumbing or electrical system recently, some companies might also provide a price break.

8. *See if you can get group coverage.* Does your employer administer a group insurance program? Check to see if a home insurance policy is available and is a better deal than you can find elsewhere. In addition, professional, alumni, and business groups might offer an insurance package at a reduced price.

9. *Stay with the same insurer.* If you've been insured with the same company for several years, you might receive a discount for being a long-term policyholder. Some insurers will reduce premiums by 5 percent if you stay with them for three to five years and by 10 percent if you're a policyholder for six years or more. To ensure that you're getting a good deal, periodically compare this price with the prices of policies from other insurers.

10. *Look for private insurance if you are in a government plan.* If you live in a high-risk area—one that is especially vulnerable to coastal storms, fires, or crime—and you've been buying your home insurance through a government plan, find out from insurance agents or your state department of insurance which insurance companies might be interested in your business. You might find there are steps you can take that will allow you to buy insurance at a lower price in the private market.

# MAKING CLAIMS: YOU BETTER GET A CLUE

You might also be paying high home insurance premiums if you've made a lot of home insurance claims within the past five years. Did you know that there's a database that tracks how many claims you've made on your home insurance policy, and in some cases, might even show your phone calls to your home insurer as claims?

Ninety percent of home insurers subscribe to CLUE, which stands for Comprehensive Loss Underwriting Exchange, a database of home-owners' claims histories. When you apply for a home insurance policy, the insurer requests a CLUE report to determine whether you have filed any claims during the past five years and whether you and your current home (or a home you might want to buy) are good insurance risks—if not, you can be denied coverage.

It happens like this: You call your insurer because you discover a leaky pipe in your bathroom and you're wondering whether it's covered. It is, but because your deductible is $500, you decide to just go ahead and fix it yourself. Six months later, your washing machine hose bursts while you're at work and you come home to find water covering your basement floor. This time, you do file a claim. A year later, you get a job transfer, put your house up for sale, and at the 11th hour, the prospective buyers back out because they can't get an insurance policy for the home because it has a "history" of water problems!

One claim is a *history?* What you don't realize is that your home insurer opened a claim file on the leaky pipe as soon as you called and then later marked it "closed, with no payment" when you decided to fix the leak yourself. Insurers say it is standard procedure to record such telephone inquiries in this manner. However, these "closed, with no payment" files show up as claims in the CLUE database.

Home insurers have relied on information from CLUE's property and casualty database (there is also one for auto claims) since its

**Clued-In:** CLUE's database tracks 27 "causes of loss" showing why a claim was submitted to a property/casualty insurer for payment, including contamination, damage to property of others, dog bite, earthquake, fire, flood, freezing water, hail, lightning, medical payment, slip/fall, smoke, theft/burglary, vandalism, water damage, and wind.

For $9, you can access your CLUE report via the Internet from ChoicePoint, the company that owns the CLUE database. (You can't order a CLUE report on a home that you don't own.) The ChoicePoint Web site is located at *http://www.choicetrust.com.*

launch in 1992. Originally, insurers used it as a background check on applicants to ferret out a pattern of fraudulent claims, according to Jeanne Salvatore, vice president of consumer affairs at the Insurance Information Institute. "What's new is that insurers are now taking a look at individual structures to see if there have been a lot of claims made on the property itself," she says.

Just like previous claims on your auto insurance policy will hike your rates or perhaps cause an insurer to refuse to renew your policy, previous claims on your home insurance policy can affect your ability to obtain coverage on a new home, or at least cause the premiums on your current home to double, even triple.

It pays to educate yourself about home insurance when you're shopping for affordable coverage for your home. Here are some ways you can help yourself:

- *Consider paying for small losses out of your own pocket.* Insurers take notice of customers who submit too many small claims. If someone breaks into your home and steals your new stereo that you bought for $400, it might just be better to go out and buy a new one at your own expense, particularly if you've had a claim or two within the past three years.

- *Think twice before you call your agent or insurance company.* If you are considering filing a claim but aren't sure, wait to make that call. The minute your insurer's customer service representative types in your name to log your call, the insurer opens a file on you that is tracked through its computer system.

- *Check your credit record.* In addition to using your past claims history, insurers will use your credit score to help them decide whether to issue you an auto or home insurance policy, where allowed by state law. In Texas, for example, Allstate Insurance Co. stopped selling new home insurance policies in 2002 to Texas consumers who rank in the bottom three tiers of the insurer's five-tier credit scoring system.

  You should order a copy of your credit record periodically to ensure that it doesn't contain mistakes that could prevent you from obtaining a home insurance policy or that will cause your insurer to raise your premiums.

# CHAPTER 13

# SELLING YOUR REMODELED HOME

# A WINNING FORMULA

Let's revisit Chapter 2 for a moment. We said that how much you recoup on your remodeling investment depends on a variety of factors. Indeed, the scope and quality of the work, the property values in your neighborhood, and the amount of time that has elapsed since your last big project all have an impact on your return when it comes time to sell.

But there are two other important factors in your investment: Curb appeal and hearth appeal. In order to maximize your return (regardless of whether your remodeling project wrapped up seven months or seven *years* ago), you must learn what all savvy real estate pros already know. Curb appeal lures potential buyers into your home, and hearth appeal closes the deal. Without them, your home can languish on the market despite brisk sales of similar homes in your neighborhood. What's worse is that a lack of one or the other (or both) can wind up knocking off anywhere from $5000 to $15,000, or more, from your asking price.

# TIPS FOR CREATING CURB APPEAL

Anything that improves the appearance of your home's exterior, including your yard, adds to your home's curb appeal. Sprucing up the outside of your home doesn't necessarily have to cost you a lot of money—it just requires you to be able to look at your home through a potential buyer's eyes and make changes accordingly.

And it's often easier said than done.

For example, what do you see when you look at the sunflowers you and your daughter planted by the garage and the several bicycles and sporting equipment strewn on the lawn near the front steps? Chances are good that you see an idyllic domestic scene and a home so welcoming that all the neighborhood children feel comfortable gathering there. But chances are equally good (if not greater) that the prospective buyer sees an unkempt tangle of tall weeds choking the drainpipe and a pile of junk in your front yard looking like a lawsuit just waiting to happen.

You get the idea. Put away your nostalgia and take a hard look around. Then make sensible changes that you're dedicated to keeping until your home sells. These include:

- Keep your lawn mowed and green in warmer months by regular watering.

- Prune shrubs, especially those around windows and doors to provide more light inside and safer access through entrances.

- Stow outside clutter such as bicycles, children's toys, grills, sporting equipment, tools, and machinery.

- If you have a garage, park your cars in it. Cars left in the driveway, or parked on the street, diminish your home's curb appeal.

- Plant flowers along walkways or around a lamppost. Place flower-pots on a porch or deck. (Don't obstruct doors or stairs.)

- Make sure the outside of your windows are sparkling clean.

- Install a doorknocker if you don't have one or fix the one that you have if it's broken. Make sure the doorbell and all door latches are in good working order.

- Affix your house number so it is visible from the street or replace any numbers that are broken or missing.

- Repair and/or paint window shutters as needed.

- Keep steps in good repair, swept, and free from clutter.

- Make sure cement walkways or patios are free from cracks. Likewise, brick walkways and patios should be smooth and level, with no bricks that are pushed up, broken, or missing.

- All exterior lighting, including porch lights and lampposts, should be in good working order.
- Put out a new "Welcome" mat.

# TIPS FOR CREATING HEARTH APPEAL

Curb appeal entices buyers into your home. Hearth appeal keeps them there—long enough to make you an offer. Whether that offer will come close to your asking price depends in part on whether your remodeled home meets a potential buyer's three most important criteria:

1. *Your home is spacious* (that means free from clutter).
2. *Your home is clean* (and free from all pet, food, and mildew odors).
3. *Your home is solid* (no squeaking steps or loose doorknobs).

You don't have to own the Taj Mahal or be Mr. or Mrs. Clean to satisfy these requirements. Even a small home will appear larger if countertops are free from clutter. A little accumulated dust on top of a bookcase is not going to penalize you if the carpets are clean and fresh and your windows and mirrors are sparkling and free from smudges.

Other tips for increasing your home's hearth appeal include:

- Hold a tag or garage sale to eliminate unnecessary items. Be ruthless. If you haven't worn it or used it within the past two or three years, get rid of it.
- Store or sell excess furniture. Too much furniture makes a room appear smaller. It also makes it harder for potential buyers to imagine what *their* furniture would look like in your home.
- Clean and organize your closets.
- Clean your oven and all appliances. Polish chrome fixtures and surfaces.

- Clean all ceiling fans.

- Make sure all your lamps and light fixtures have working bulbs in the correct wattage.

- Tighten any loose doorknobs, switch plates, or cabinet hinges. Fix loose moldings. Replace broken cabinet hardware. Fix doors and windows that stick. Repair anything that rattles, squeaks, or leaks.

- Replace carpeting that is worn, stained, or smelly.

- Clean walls of finger smudges and crayon marks. Repaint if necessary.

- Clean and organize your basement, attic, and garage.

- Regularly empty, clean, and deodorize litter boxes. Keep them in a discreet location or behind a privacy screen.

## A WORD ABOUT HOME STAGING

The way you live in your home is quite different from the way you should market it for sale, says Barbara Schwarz, and she ought to know. After all, Schwarz is the former theater major and real estate dynamo who coined the phrase "home staging" and received the Stage® Federally Registered Trademark from the United States government in 1990.

A decade ago, few of Schwarz's clients or colleagues knew what she meant when she told them they could "set the scene" to sell their properties for top dollar. Today, after teaching more than 400,000 real estate professionals and decorators the ins and outs of Staging® a home for sale, both the phrase and the concept are accepted and commonly used throughout the real estate industry.

According to Schwarz, homeowners must "lovingly cut the strings of attachment" when it comes time to put their homes up for sale. "Buyers only know what they see—not what [the home] will be," she says. Therefore, Schwarz recommends taking down your family photographs before showing your home.

---

**TIPS FOR STAGING® YOUR HOME FOR SALE**

- Clear all unnecessary objects from furniture throughout the house.
- Clear all unnecessary objects from the kitchen countertops. Clear refrigerator fronts of messages, pictures, etc. (A sparse kitchen helps the buyer mentally move their own things into your kitchen.)
- In the bathroom, remove any unnecessary items from countertops, tubs, shower stalls, and commode tops. Keep only your most needed cosmetics, brushes, perfumes, and toiletries in one small group on the counter. Coordinate towels to one or two colors only.
- Rearrange or remove some of the furniture if necessary. You need to thin out as much as possible to make rooms appear larger.
- During "showings" turn on all lights and lamps.
- Have stereo FM playing during the day for all viewings.

Source: Stagedhome.com

---

If homeowners balk at her gentle prodding, Schwarz reminds them that, hopefully, they will be moving soon, so packing up some items in advance helps them stay ahead of the game. When there are no personal items or mementos to distract them, potential homebuyers are better able to visualize their own family enjoying the home.

# PART 5

# HOME RESOURCES

# CHAPTER 14

# THE EXPERTS

# FEATURED HOME PROFESSIONALS

Each year, the National Association of the Remodeling Industry (NARI) holds an "Evening of Excellence" that culminates with the Contractor of the Year (COTY) Awards ceremony. In 2003, 16 design/build firms were named COTY award winners. These designer/contractors represent a select group from the approximately 800,000 companies and individuals in the United States that identify themselves as remodelers. For this book, we spoke extensively with representatives from five 2003 COTY award-winning firms. These companies, their representatives, and their award-winning projects are:

- **Bath & Kitchen Creations, Inc., Fairfax, Virginia:** *Best Residential Kitchen under $15,000.* Bob Clements, president. *http://www.bathandkitchencreations.com*

- **Block Builders, Bethesda, Maryland:** *Best Residential Exterior.* Tony Paulos, president. *http://www.blockbuilders.com/*

- **Capital Improvements, Allen, Texas:** *Best Residential Kitchen $30,000 to $60,000 and Best Residential Addition $100,000 and Under.* Paul Zuchs, president. *http://www.cimprovements.com*

- **Dreammaker Bath and Kitchen, St Louis Park, Minnesota:** Best *Residential Kitchen $15,000 to $30,000.* A.J. Paron-Wildes, general manager. *http://www.dreammaker-remodel.com/*

- **Neal's Remodeling, Cincinnati, Ohio.** *Best Entire Home Remodeling.* Steve Hendy, owner. *http://www.neals.com*

Other leading home professionals we interviewed for this book include:

- **David Adams** of David Adams Design, Building, and Remodeling was named Fairfield County's "Remodeler of the Year" in 2003.

All projects submitted to the COTY contest must be an improvement or an addition to an existing structure. New construction projects are ineligible. Judging is based on problem solving, functionality, aesthetics, craftsmanship, innovation, degree of difficulty, and entry presentation.

He has a kitchen and bath showroom in Ridgefield, Connecticut and he offers full design services, including excavation, tiling, and painting.

- Stephen Gladstone is the owner and president of Stonehollow, Inc. Fine Homes Inspections (*http://www.stonehollow.com*) and is currently serving as the president of the American Society of Home Inspectors (ASHI). He is host of *Around the House*, a weekly radio program in Norwalk, Conn.

- **Alan Hanbury,** a frequent building industry speaker, is the treasurer of House of Hanbury Builders, a full service remodeling company in Newington, Conn. House of Hanbury Builders was inducted into Remodeling Magazine's "Big 50" Hall of Fame in 1992 and was named "Remodeler of the Year" for Connecticut in 1994.

- **Barbara Schwarz ,** a former Seattle real estate professional, is a seasoned speaker with more than 12,000 hours on the platform She is internationally known as the creator of Staging® and a best-selling real estate author. Her video, *How to Prepare Your Home for Sale So It Sells,* won the Consumer Education Product of the Year Award from the Real Estate Educators of America.

- **Carl Seville** is the vice president of SawHorse Inc., Atlanta's largest design/build full-service residential remodeling firm. He is also a columnist for Housingzone.com. *http://www.sawhorse.net*

- **Don Woods** is president of the Stonehedge Landscaping & Garden Center, Inc. Stonehedge is a full-service design-build landscape architecture firm, specializing in residential, commercial, and institutional landscaping. Stonehedge is a preferred contractor for the Professional Golf Assocation's course at River Highlands in Cromwell, Conn.

# RELATED WEB SITES

The Internet is a do-it-yourselfer's paradise: There are countless articles and nuggets of information to provide you with guidance on your home improvement journey. If you want to learn more about how to increase the value of your home, please stop by and visit Dan and Vicki at *www.addhomevalue.com*. You'll find the latest news and information about home improvement trends and tips from the experts.

In addition, the following Web sites are helpful:

- *www.aarp.org/universalhome*: Plans and information for a universal home designed for people of all ages.

- *www.abathroomguide.com*: Billing itself as "A bathroom guide – innovative ideas for your bathroom," this Web site contains design tips, product ideas and an online calculator.

- *abc.go.com/primetime/xtremehome/*: Home improvement with a heart and a hunk.

- *www.anla.org*: The American Nursery & Landscape Association is the national voice of the nursery and landscape industry.

- *www.americanlightingassoc.com*: The ALA is an organization of lighting manufacturers, showrooms, and sales representatives dedicated to providing the public with quality residential lighting.

- *www.bobvila.com*: Information and tips about home improvement projects from Bob Vila's *Home Again* television show.

- *tlc.discovery.com/fansites/cleansweep/cleansweep.html*: *Clean Sweep* is a packrat's nightmare, but very entertaining TV.

- *doityourself.com*: Detailed home improvement tips about a variety of home improvement projects.
- *www.energystar.gov*: A government Web site that helps you decide how to build improvements with energy efficiency in mind.
- *www.eere.energy.gov/erec/factsheets/landscape.html*: A government Web site about landscaping for energy efficiency.
- *www.hgtv.com*: The place to go to learn more about the programs and projects featured on Home and Garden Television.
- *www.homedepot.com*: The Web site for the largest home improvement retailer in the world.
- *www.hometime.com*: Online resource for the popular television show.
- *www.hometips.com*: A one-stop resource for help with home improvement, remodeling houses, home repair, decorating, and buying appliances and other home products.
- *www.ibhs.org*: The Institute for Business and Home Safety is a nonprofit association that educates members about reducing losses from natural disasters.
- *www.iii.org*: The Insurance Information Institute is the place to go on the Web to find out about insurance and how it works.
- *www.improvenet.com*: Online calculators help give you a ballpark cost estimate of different home improvements in your zip code.
- *kitchens.com*: Design, photos, and tips for your kitchen remodeling job.
- *landscaping.about.com*: Resources than help you develop, design, and build your next landscaping home improvement project.
- *www.lowes.com:* The Web site for Lowe's, the world's second-largest home improvement retailer.
- *www.nari.org:* The National Association of the Remodeling Industry (NARI) represents contractors, design-build firms,

manufacturers, suppliers, distributors, subcontractors, lenders, and other related professionals who work in the remodeling field.

- *www.nari.org/level2/awards*: National Contractor of the Year (COTY) award-winning projects may be viewed here.

- *www.nfpa.org/catalog/home/index.asp*: The mission of the National Fire Protection Association is to reduce the worldwide burden of fire and other hazards.

- *www.ourfamilyplace.com/homeseller*: The Home Seller's Information Center strives to take the mystery out of selling your home.

- *www.realtor.org*: The Web site for the National Association of REALTORS®.

- *tlc.discovery.com/fansites/tradingspaces/tradingspaces.html*: The Web site for *Trading Spaces,* TLC's popular home improvement show.

- *www.thisoldhouse.com/toh/*: The landmark series that started it all more than 20 years ago.

- *tlc.discovery.com/fansites/wywo/wywo.html*: *While You Were Out,* another popular home makeover show from TLC.

- *www.wfca.org*: The World Floor Covering Association is the industry's largest trade organization representing specialty floor covering retailers, manufacturers, and distributors.

# INDEX

# ABOUT THE AUTHORS

**Vicki Lankarge** (West Hartford, CT) is an authority on protecting the value of houses. Her writing on consumer issues appears on aol.com, CBS Marketwatch, and MSN.com.

**Dan Nahorney** (Newington, CT) a long-time weekend home improvement warrior, is a journalist, business writer, and magazine editor.